Magic Dimensions

Magic Dimensions

Personal Transformations Through Magic, Miracles and Quantum Mechanics

Dave R. Oester, D.D., Ph.D. and Sharon A. Gill, Ph.D.

Writers Club Press
San Jose New York Lincoln Shanghai

Magic Dimensions
Personal Transformations Through Magic, Miracles and Quantum Mechanics

Writers Club Press
an imprint of iUniverse, Inc.

For information address:
iUniverse, Inc.
5220 S. 16th St., Suite 200
Lincoln, NE 68512
www.iuniverse.com

ISBN: 0-595-22032-0

Printed in the United States of America

This book is dedicated to all those who want to believe in magic and to those who have helped us gain a greater understanding of life's magic along the way.

Contents

List of Contributors

Herbert Isaacs

Anne Marie Jamieson

Shaun-Marie Newcomer

Laura Olmsted

Linda Pendergrass

Marshall Philyaw

Jeff Reynolds

Sue Sereno

Ned Stevens

Donald Swain

J. Maciej Trojanowski

David Weaver

Chanda Wright

Introduction

This book is about personal transformation caused by undesirable changes in our health, employment, finances, relationships or other personal areas. We will show how personal transformations can occur through magic, miracles and quantum mechanics. Magic is real if you believe in it and through magic miracles are caused to happen and through miracles we can understand the workings of quantum mechanics. Follow us as we journey through the magic found in the Native American pathway that is called the Red Road. Explore the magic of pagan witchcraft and how it connects to early Christianity. The Dead Sea Scrolls reveals the ancient Language of Prayer and how it is interwoven into magical rituals and parallel dimensions.

In the Beginning

The story begins in December 2000 when we made the decision to pack our household belongings into storage units and hit the road full time traveling in our twenty-one-foot RV (Recreational Vehicle). We would be known as "Full Timers" by the more than one million people who travel and live full time in their Recreational Vehicles. We both love to travel and to see what is over the next mountain and around the next bend in the road. Unlike Snowbird's who travel four to six months out of the year, we elected to travel full time in our RV or Rig. Our backyard became the good old USA as we traveled from the Pacific to the Atlantic and then back to the Pacific.

Along the way we discovered we were not just sight seeing or investigating America's most haunted sites, but we were beginning a spiritual odyssey into the world of magic. We were led to people and places that helped us understand the purpose of our magical spiritual odyssey. In the following pages, we are sharing our insights and perspicacity made along the way. The catalysts for this transformation were the first two books in the popular Harry Potter series by J. K. Rowling. Some may consider Rowling's books written for children, but this misconception is soon forgotten as adults become trapped in the magical web. Her writing style and story line has captured the attention of adults as well. The author weaves a tale of a magical world where mystical creatures, spells and the constant battles against the dark forces are fought. It is a right brain world where all things are possible. We realized that magic is the natural way as Harry Potter attends the Hogwart School for Witchcraft and Wizardry. The books stimulated the imagination within us again and we found the magical stories seemed to unlock hidden caverns of the mind. A world of magic that has been long forgotten.

It was during the reading of these magical tales that a spark was ignited within us that grew into a raging fire. We knew that there was something more in life and that it had to do with magic. We believed in magic and realized there was more truth to those Harry Potter's books than met the eye. We felt that we had to know more. This was really the beginning of our spiritual odyssey, which was to be, in part, the search for magic. Little did we realize that our search for magic would lead us toward the discovery of a magical doorway that anyone can pass through. A gateway that allows us to transcend time and space.

The objective of this book is to present unique insights and reveal protocols for initiating personal transformational or dimensional changes by investigating the ancient pagan theologies that encourage positive transformation for its disciples. We will also discuss the relational issues surrounding Christianity and the nature-based pagan theology. Each facet that we teach is not new or revolutionary, but imparts a different prospective and understanding to the interconnectedness of all things.

Unlike the traditional approach to personal transformational changes, we are suggesting there exists a methodology that personal transformational changes can be accomplished by the direct application of magic, miracles and quantum mechanics. Join us as we explore the four pathways consisting of the Red Road, Pagan Witchcraft, Christianity and Quantum Mechanics and how these are all interconnected. We will share with the reader, the protocols for initiating the magical personal transformation within their lives.

Down the Red Road

We had been extended an invitation to stay with one of our ghost club members, David Weaver of Quarryville, Pennsylvania, after our hosting of the annual Gettysburg Ghost Conference. He had a large level site for us to park our RV at his home and plenty of room for our dog to run and play. His home was nestled in the woods where it was quiet and peaceful which was exactly what we needed. We decided to take him up on his generous offer and after the conference, spent the next ten days enjoying the peaceful, wooded beauty of his property. It was here, over the best coffee in the county, that we learned about the Red Road that David Weaver is following.

The Red Road is a term used for those individuals who want to follow their hearts and respect the earth, after the manner of the American Indians. The important facet of the Red Road is that the color of skin is not significant because beneath the skin, we are all the same color. The primary philosophical teaching is that we are all brothers and sisters living on this planet and we need to learn to respect and care for the planet, as if she was alive. In their teachings, all who are native to this land, meaning anyone who was born in the United States, is a Native American.

David Weaver dwells near forest land that for the last two hundred years, his father and the fathers before him have called home. It is said that anyone who has roots that extend back several hundred years in that area will find Indian blood by marriage. David Weaver, or as he calls himself, "CuppaJO" always has a pot of coffee (JO) brewing for visitors. Facts be known, David Weaver makes some of the best coffee we have ever tasted.

In the secluded woods behind his house, he has constructed a sweat lodge for observing the ceremonies and rituals of his chosen pathway. David took us on that path by leading us down a forest trail that twisted and turned around trees and up a small hill to a small clearing in the woods. Set within a small stone circle was his sweat lodge. Each of the stones in the circle has a special significance to David because each stone had been brought from other sweat lodges and placed there by those who attended the Sweat Lodge Ceremonies. The Sweat Lodge Ceremony traditionally is used for many purposes, such as cleansing body, mind and spirit and for vision quests.

We were privileged to attend a workshop conducted by Silverchain, a Native American who spoke of the history of his people and how the great mother turtle rose out of the sea to form the island we call America today. The concept of the great mother turtle is part of the Water Diver mythology that is found in almost all Indian tribes, except for the Pacific Northwest and the American Southwest. Silverchain's tale of the great mother turtle reflected the mythology that his people hold sacred which explains the creation process.

The traditional story of the Water Diver has an animal that dives into the water and brings forth mud or in the case of the turtle, its shell that rose to the surface to create the land. Some tribes have the duck as the creature that brought forth the mud to create the land. In those tribes, the duck is held in esteem and can be found as the central icon in the carving of their calumet or peace pipe. The duck and the turtle would be representative of the creation of the land found in the Book of Genesis. The Water Diver mythology plays a very important role in providing the understanding of how land came to be, often representing the Mother Earth.

Silverchain was of the Wolf Clan and is a member of the Mohawk Nation within the Iroquois Confederacy. He was also known as Hyhotah. He spoke about the value and importance of following your heart, or as they say, the "red road." Hyhotah is a descendant of Chinichchuk who escaped the genocide of the Paxton boys in Conestoga and at the

Lancaster jail. He said that everyone born in America is Native American, though most of us don't think of things that way. The message he spoke about was the importance of respecting our planet and following our hearts. Hyhotah was a dynamic speaker who spoke from his heart as he told the stories of his people. He said the white man says, "I think" while the red man says, "I feel!"

David Weaver follows the Kalpulli system which is promulgated by Tlakaelel, an Aztec Elder. Kalpulli means that all members are equal in the group. There is no leader, no power positions, no one reigning over another, only people among their peers. All are respected and honored as this was the ancient way as taught by the Aztec Elder. We learned of the Sun Dance Ceremony and the rituals involved for those who strive to become Sun Dancers in preparation to one day become Medicine Men. The importance of their rituals and chants were observed first hand as we saw how chants influence behavior in rituals. Those who follow the Red Road are not trying to be Indians, but they are seeking the spiritual pathway followed by the many generations of different tribes.

David Weaver showed us how he honored the land by administering his woods as a refuge for wildlife and for those individuals seeking direction or resolution in their lives. He believes he is the steward of the land, to care for it and share it with all who wish to enjoy its beauty. Many visitors come to walk in the silence of the woods or to experience the sweat lodge. It is here in the solitude of the woods that seekers find the answers to their questions. Here there are no clocks, no schedules, no rat race, but instead there is to be found the beautiful serenity of nature. Those with open hearts will find spiritual guidance and come away with a deeper understanding of our responsibility as stewards of this world.

We asked David Weaver to express some of his thoughts regarding following the Red Road. He shared these thoughts with us.

Within every being is a spark, a spirit, a soul. This is that part of the Great Mystery that created us all. Since we were loved enough to be created in the first place, this makes us all very special and as important as all the universe. One should never look into the starlit sky and feel small, like a tiny speck, because our spirit is as bright as any star or galaxy. Within each of our hearts, our spirits, is contained all the universal truths.

Often, these truths are sleeping within us because of the society from which we are raised within, a religion, of family practice or belief. This spirit within is part of the sacred circle of life and all around us is part of the same. From the smallest things we can see and not see, to the grandest mountain, and all in our universe. We are all-important links in this chain of Creation. When one breaks or is weak, then we all are effected. We all have red blood and our hearts are red as well. So the Good Red Road is this circle of life.

Walking the Red Road has nothing to do with race, culture, or where we live on Mother Earth. The Red Road is a way of walking through this gift of life on this beautiful Earth Mother. It sounds simple but can be a very difficult thing to do. Because we are taught in most societies to disregard our hearts and allow our heads to lead, we doubt ourselves, our gut feelings we say. The Good Red Road is following your heart, walking in a balance with all that is around us (all life), and being human beings. It is allowing our heart to govern our minds. How often do we feel something in our hearts but allow our heads to decide? Even when we know in our hearts that what we have decided and acted upon, shouldn't have been. Then we say, I knew I shouldn't have done this or that.

How many times do we go by the roses and not take the time to smell the wonderful aromas of our grand gift of life? When we walk in the balance, which is an ongoing process, and we listen to all around us, we will hear things. We will be guided and helped and energized. An Aztec Elder, friend, and teacher named Tlakaelel, told me that all the trees are like the Internet. That all their roots are connected and their branches connected. And if you pray by a tree, or want to communicate with someone on the other side of the world, the trees can help you. The animals, insects, fish, birds, plants, trees, and even the rocks can help you. They can help you if you listen and not only with your ears but with your heart. There are voices in the wind. I know it sounds strange and crazy to some but, once you are on the Red Road, you can't go back to what you knew before. You can get one of your feet outside your path but you can't leave, even when you feel hopeless and down. Once you have experienced and listened, you feel the connection with all things in the universe.

Many believe that humans are superior to all other life forms, but what would happen to humans if all the plants would be gone tomorrow? Humans would die. If all humans were to be gone tomorrow the plants would thrive better than they do at present. But it is not a question of whom or what is superior but that we are all part of this organism called Earth. We are her children and all depend and sacrifice for each other in order to live.

It has been said by Chief Seattle, "Whatever we do to the Earth, we do to ourselves." When the Earth is sick, so is her children. Religions are not bad things, at least those that promote love and equality aren't bad. But this should extend to all of life and all of our universe. I was raised in the Christian faith but it could not answer the endless quest for knowledge and understanding. This drive is always with me and will always be. No answers are set in stone and some great mysteries cannot be answered. And I cannot accept any belief that states, "we are the one and only." The quest is in the nature of us humans and all religions and beliefs have only a part of the truth.

The Good Red Road is love and love is the most powerful force in the Universe. I believe it is the force that created the Universe. I believe that total and pure love is the Great Mystery, The Great Spirit, The Creator, The Universal Intelligence. We can love and understand, at least in part, it's great power. I believe that Jesus was telling people to look inside their hearts. That all I can do you can do as well. Look within and you will see. It is not one thing or one person or one belief. The path of The Good Red Road is key to unlocking the mysteries and truths that lie within us all. That lie within every leaf and rock.

Dr. Albert Schweitzer once said, "Until he extends his circle of compassion to all living things, man himself will not find peace." Some people in all walks of life and religions and lands are on the Good Red Road. They speak in actions and example through their love. This blessed nation of the U.S.A. has a spirit unlike any in the world. It comes from the spirit of those native people that have lived here for thousands upon thousands of years.

When the Spaniards invaded this land over 500 years ago, it was a garden of Eden and had been all those thousands of years. The reason

being that these indigenous people, followed the Good Red Road. They respected this land. I revel in the privilege that I am part of this great web of life, as tiny a strand that I may be. That I am as important as the next. My very existence is proof of this. I am loved enough to have been created, as you, and as everything.

The Good Red Road is The Balance. All is equal and important in this Balance. It is not the size of our brains but that spark of spirit that makes us one with all. There are so many voices to hear. There are so many senses besides the five we use. So many things we cannot see outside of our own dimension. The walk the way of the Red Road opens our minds and hearts, it energizes our vision. Our spirits are trapped inside these physical bodies, at this time, in this dimension.

The Good Red Road allows us to be who we are. There are no pattern, example or rules to follow. The leader is the heart, the spirit, the spark, the love. It is all things. Each day is a wonderful gift yet we live so fast today that things are a blur as we go flying by. Looking within is seeing outside of ourselves.

◆   ◆   ◆

Even in this Garden of Eden, there are those who dance to the beat of a different drum. As with any philosophy there are extreme views held by individuals who insist that there is only one way to do a ceremony or ritual and if it is not followed to the letter, then it is flawed. We found that there are Red Road fundamentalists who have extreme and rigid views on how ceremonies or rituals are to be conducted. Those fundamentalists believe that the ritual is the most important aspect of the ceremony and any deviation can cause the ceremony to be void as a futile waste of time. They believe the primary importance is the ritual act, not the words uttered in the chant. This is contrary to other tribes who hold the spoken word as more important than the ritual itself. We found the various philosophies encompassing the path of the Red Road were different, but not to the extent that bitter contentions were directed toward others.

On the Red Road path, we find both the fundamentalist and the conservative. For example, on the conservative side, we find the Oglala Sioux who follow the vision of the seer and medicine man, Black Elk. Their holy men each perform the ceremonies a little differently, unique unto his own way. Perhaps the colors they use are a little different or the order of the four colors are arranged in a different way. According to the Oglala Sioux, the importance about *Black Elk Speaks*, is not the absolute construct spoken about, but the vision that he presented to his people.

Beyond learning about the pathway known as the Red Road, we felt that we were meant to be among these wonderful people at this time, not only to recharge our batteries and refresh ourselves, but to learn more about the pathway followed by the Indians. We experienced a great peacefulness there. The people we met who followed the Red Road were at peace within themselves. One young man named Chris Thompson demonstrated his skills with the flute and we could immediately see he is destined for greatness, such as flutist R. Carlos Nakai or Douglas Spotted Eagle.

Our study of religious rituals triggered some interesting insights. We especially noted the spiritual relationship that these chants, rituals and ceremonies had to the Language of Prayer and of shifting into other realities or dimensions. When it came time to depart, David Weaver honored us by presenting us with a handmade deer horn rattle, made by him in the traditional way, for use in the rituals and chants to help us remember the way of the Red Road. We left Quarryville, Pennsylvania rested and filled with a new understanding and respect for those who walk the Red Road.

What did we learn? We learned that the American Indians view all things as having spiritual energy and value. All things are connected, all things have life and all things are worthy of respect and reverence. Their spiritual beliefs focus on the necessity of harmony and balance by emphasizing that everything is alive, has a purpose, is connected and all can embrace the Medicine of all living things as they walk together in the circle. This concept is known by many names, such as the *Medicine Way, Natural Way* and *Red Road* to name a few. The Circle of Life consists of nature, body, mind and spirit. The term "Medicine" means way of life. The Indians believe that a person's Medicine is his or her power and this duality can be used for creative or destructive purposes.

Their Circle is a sacred reminder of the interrelationship, respect, and cohesion that come from opening oneself up to the energy of the Circle of Life. The vision given to Black Elk was about the Sacred Hoops representing circles within circles or the interconnectedness of all things. The circle is an important aspect to all expressions of daily life. Their individual teepee's would be laid out in conjunction with other teepee's forming a circle to represent the Circle of Life. The Indians knew how to show respect and honor to all living things that their European white brothers had failed to learn. They did not judge one another based on possessions, but upon being human. They had no poor as all were treated with respect. The widows and infirmed were allocated rations from each hunters' kill, so none went hungry. The tribe took care of their own completely.

While visiting Pipestone, Minnesota, we came upon the great quarry where the red pipestone is dug by hand and used for carving the sacred peace pipes. Buffalo Calf Woman spoke about this when she gave the Indians the Sacred Pipe Ceremony as part of the seven sacred ceremonies. Once again we found ourselves led to the one and only site in the United States where the red pipestone is quarried. It wasn't the direction we had intended to take and yet the circumstances surrounding us at the time, took us to a place we needed to be, to learn and grow more in Native wisdom.

The red pipestone peace pipe is the highest honor that can be bestowed on a tribal member. The experience for us was just another in a long trail of singular events that helped us to understand the spirituality of those who follow the nature-based ways of life and beliefs. We purchased some red pipestone from the Oglala Sioux and will one day carve our own pipe from it.

The ceremonies and rituals conducted by the Oglala Sioux reinforced the importance of rituals and ceremonies in the expression of their belief system. They call anyone who is not of red skin, "rainbow" as spoken about as the rainbow of colors in Black Elks' vision. The Oglala Sioux invite all to follow that vision, which they feel is what is needed to heal the earth and to become interconnected with everyone else. We met a Cheyenne woman in Pipestone who was fulfilling her assignment from ten years before, as she selected a red pipestone block that she intended to carve for her peace pipe.

The peace pipe is used in the Sweat Lodge Ceremony and for each of the other sacred ceremonies and rituals that members perform. When the peace pipe is not in use, the peace pipe is broken down by removing the stem from the bowl and each is carried separately. The two pieces come together symbolizing the masculine and feminine energies for rituals. Until the time the two pieces are united, the bowl and stem are separate and without purpose. They become as one, in balance and wholeness, when brought together. Again we have the duality represented by the male and female energies. This represents the duality of nature and of our existence upon the earth. While this may represent duality in the form of icons, it is a sacred understanding reinforced each time the peace pipe is used in ceremonies, by the Indians.

As the late Joseph Campbell taught, the American Indian mythologies demonstrated the importance of values, such as merit, respect and morality. Their stories are illustrated by the introduction of talking animals who taught lessons needed by their people. These stories were handed down from generation to generation. Their sacred stories told of the creation of this planet, the creation of life and their responsibility to honor the land they walked upon. The animals in their tales represented the animals that the Indians came into contact with every day. Something of a physical nature that they could relate to as an icon. The Plain Indians revered the Buffalo as it sustained them with food and clothing. The Pacific Northwest Indians revered the Salmon because it was the staple of their diet. Each culture respected and honored the creatures that provided them with the food or clothing that they needed to sustain their lives. In return, they honored them, thanking them for their sacrifice.

The American Indians had ceremonies and rituals that enabled them to develop a more spiritual relationship with their God. These rituals enabled them to transcend the physical and enter the spiritual realm. Their ceremonies and rituals were considered pagan because they did not have to take place within four walls. Indians did not live within four walls because it blocked the flow of energy whereas the circle did not. Their rituals and ceremonies were held within sacred circles, the circular sweat lodge, or within a circle of stones. They conducted their rituals, dancing almost to exhaustion, as they prepared to enter an altered state of consciousness that would enable them to transcend the physical realm. The rituals were almost hypnotic as the individual members continued until they entered their altered states. It is while within these altered states that visions and guidance came to them. It must be noted that most Indians do not approve of the use of drugs to induce these altered states.

The transmigration of sacred Indian allegories can be compared to the allegories of the Bible and how they were assembled. The Indians passed verbal knowledge down from generation to generation, such as the Mother Turtle myth wherein the people were are taught to respect and honor women and Mother Earth. Women were honored because they brought forth life. Before a tribe could go to war, the "Grandmother" or Matriarch was consulted, before the Chief decreed war. Many of the Indian beliefs dealt with the sacredness of women and mothers, unlike their counterparts in the Bible. In fact women were very much looked down upon in the Scriptures, for what was thought to be, good reasons of that time period. St. Peter described women as, "the weaker vessel."

The Church father, Tertullian expressed feelings about women a bit stronger. Women were said to deserve their status of being despised and inferior. According to Tertullian, "And do you not know that you are an Eve? The sentence of God on this sex of yours lives in this age: the guilt must of necessity live too. You are the devil's gateway: you are the unsealer of that tree: you are the first deserter of the divine law: you are she who persuaded him whom the devil was not valiant enough to attack. You destroyed so easily God's image, man. On account of your desert-that is, death-even the Son of God had to die."

In the Consolation of Philosophy, the Christian philosopher, Boethius wrote, "Woman is a temple built upon a sewer." In the sixth century, the Council of Macon voted to determine whether women even had souls. In the tenth century, Odo of Cluny stated that, "To embrace a woman is to embrace a sack of manure." Even St. Thomas Acquinas, in the thirteenth century suggested that perhaps God had made a mistake in the creating of women. A reference to the Bible Apocrypha says that, "Of woman came the beginning of sin and thanks to her, we all must die."

In I Corinthians 7:1 it says, "It is a good thing for a man to have nothing to do with a woman." Christians found fault and placed blame on women for any number of reasons. In the thirteenth century a Dominican stated that woman is "the confusion of man, an insatiable beast, a continuous anxiety, an incessant warfare, a daily ruin, a house of tempest…a hindrance to devotion."

The only mention of the sacred nature of women is in the Joseph and Mary account. Each culture has its own mythology that plays a powerful role in establishing standards and protocols for its members. Women were little more than slaves in the service of men and they had no position in society. With the onset of the witch hunts, formalized by Pope John XXII in 1320, it has been found that between 80-90% of the thousands deemed guilty of witchcraft, was women.

Pagan Witchcraft

The next stop on our spiritual odyssey was to learn more about the pagan beliefs and magic ceremonies that predated the Christian era. We can learn much from the study of pagan religions. Their respect for the earth and all living things is like an oasis in the desert. Pagan means "country dweller" and country dwellers were those people who were the farmers, cattlemen, sheep herders and those whose existence revolved around an agricultural-based society. Their religion was based on nature and natures icons. Pagan worship, from the beginning was as natural for them as it is today for organized religions to hold services inside physical structures. As the Christian Church expanded, their beliefs were forced onto the local people they conquered. The problem was the local people still celebrated their own Pagan holidays, so the Church simply absorbed those holidays, declaring them to be Christian holidays. The people were content as they were still celebrating their version of the Pagan holiday as they always had. There are many claims that suggest most, if not all, of the rituals of Christendom, were taken from original pagan ceremonies.

We were given the opportunity of learning first hand about a pagan, earth-based religion known as Wicca which is perhaps the largest nature-based religion in the United States and the United Kingdom. We were introduced to three solitary witches who practice the magic art. These are not the cauldron stirring, broom riding variety of witches, but the kinds who work spells for healing and helping others, and who follow the Three Fold Law. The ancient Sage, Hermes Trismegistus, wrote down a law that says that anything you send out will be returned to you threefold. Today we might call this the Law of the Boomerang or what goes around, comes around.

Admittedly, the concept of what you send forth comes back to you three fold may not be understood by scientists today, but fifty years ago very few scientists understood quantum mechanics and parallel dimensions. Why something is returned three fold may lie in the understanding of how the space-time fabric functions regarding dimensional shifting. However, this concept is not as important as the concept of "As ye harm none, do what you will." This is the primary edict that witches obey and can be compared to the Ten Commandments. As long as you are harming no one than you can do what you will. Wicca does not acknowledge the Christian concept of Original Sin nor the need for baptism. The earth-based beliefs lie outside the need for a church building, a priesthood and of redemption from the Original Sin.

Perhaps this polarity is the focal point for the abomination felt by the Christian churches and it's membership toward those who practice witchcraft. Witchcraft does not accept Christian teachings and therefore have no need for the Church or its influence in their lives. Even today, the term "witchcraft" rakes the gull of fundamentalists and conservatives alike. Some who follow pagan beliefs find themselves watchful of Christian zealots who might take it upon themselves to strike out at them, as was done during the Witch Hunts of the Middle Ages and in Salem Massachusetts in 1692. What is most sad is that before the onset and growth of the Christian religion, witches were respected and revered as healers and seers. They were turned to for help by all, even those within royalty depended upon their talents for healing their ailments and foreseeing future events and outcomes. We found that those who live their beliefs and practice their religion in silence are gentle and loving people, very much misunderstood. They focus on the healing of those who are sick and advocate positive thinking and positive action.

Witchcraft was simply the craft or the techniques employed in the practice of their religion which focused on honoring and respecting life, having nothing to do with Satanic worship or human sacrifices.

Those who teach that Witchcraft is Satanic are blinded by their own fears and by their lack of knowledge. But as we have traveled and researched across this great land, we have found this to be a common behavior pattern expressed by Christian people. It is easier to judge and condemn than to research and learn about something that creates fear. Hollywood films have depicted the pentagram as being Satanic symbolism, but the pentacle is inverted in the same way as the Christian cross can be inverted to have a Satanic depiction. Few Christians realize that the Christian cross can be used as a Satanic symbol in the same way as the inverted pentacle.

While visiting with a Wiccan member, we were given access to an enormous library of books written by most of the well known and respected witches from England and America. We studied the history of the Pagan craft and discovered that the Wiccan religion worships the masculine and feminine energies found in nature. Not all witches are Wiccans, but all Wiccans are witches. We found that the general term, "witch" can also be interpreted as shaman, wizard, sorcerer, magician, sage, priest, medicine man or voodoo practitioners. In its most rudimentary form, "witch" means a practitioner of magic, male or female. While some witch covens view rituals and chants in a fundamental manner and may have clear and precise interpretations, this is not true for all covens. Each coven is free to choose or reject its own creed and method of ceremonial magic.

Most of us imagine witches as brewing a nasty concoction in a cauldron under the cover of darkness. We envision them standing by a big, black, bubbling cauldron adding such terrible ingredients as eye of newt or bat wings. However, the truth is that these terrible names are the common or generic names that were given to plants and herbs that bore a resemblance to the name. This practice was also employed by the physicians in early Egypt. It was easier to remember a plant that looked like the tip of a bat's wing than to remember its more difficult, scientific label, especially for those looking to harvest these plants and herbs.

We use this same technique today by giving nicknames to things we work with. Consider gun power. In the early days, one of the ingredients was sodium nitrate, but the nickname for it was saltpeter. Witches used nicknames for healing plants and this practice spooked many people. Today in the back woods of West Virginia, Kentucky and Tennessee, one can find natural healers who use nicknames for herbs to heal the sick. We use common names or nicknames for plants and flowers all the time instead of their Latin names. It is easy for people of this day and age to forget that in ancient civilizations, education was at a minimum and most country people were not educated. To expect them to use anything but a common name for the plants they used in their work, would be ludicrous.

Once we dispel the Hollywood explanation of a witch or the Church categorizing of witches with Satanic worship and other Church sanctioned demons, we find witches to be like you and me. They are decent, loving, giving, hard-working people who practice their form of religion different from the traditional Western religions. They are not out pounding on doors or stopping people in the streets to preach and convert them, nor do they feel impelled to inquire what Church people attend. They respect other people's beliefs and practice their earth-based religion on a personal level. In Wicca, magic is most often spelled as magick when used in ritual magic and spelled magic when it is practiced by someone outside of the craft. We do not make such a separation in spelling. We use the nondescript term "magic" because to us, magic is magic.

Magic can be defined as the changing of future events by ritual procedures that use the transcendental energy from yourself and from natural sources. Be assured that none of the witches we encountered were of the Hollywood stereotypes, with warts on their long noses nor were they stirring bubbling caldrons while bat wings and eye of newt were tossed into the boiling, greenish brew. But one did have a black cat that belonged to her son, if that means anything to anyone superstitious. We did not see any goats tied in the back yard for future use either.

Unfortunately today, the term "witch" still brings negative connotations and insinuations due to the cultural imprints forced upon society by the invasive Christian church.

We were able to observe and discuss the many rituals held and the order in which they should be conducted. The importance of spells, chants and ceremonies and their relationship to the sacred circle that reminded us of the Medicine Wheel used by the Indians and those who follow the Red Road. So many of the rituals, chants, spells and tools used within the craft were similar to those used in Indian ceremonies, but called by different names. The function still served the same purpose, but the applications varied. Since all earth-based religions had a common predecessor, it is no wonder so many earth-based religions have similar rituals. This is similar to the traditional practice of rituals and rights found in the thousands of different Christian sects and how similar so many of them are to each sect. We began to see the link to link or interconnectedness of all rituals, again as circles within circles.

We have been able to relate so much of what we have learned to the Language of Prayer. The rituals, chants, spells, tools used by Indians and followers of the "Red Road" are similar to those of the Wiccan's and the Pagan practitioners. This is further evidence of a common thread that weaves throughout the different nature-based religions. We understand the concerns that Wiccan members have about their beliefs and how they are perceived by the public. Many witches still fear the repercussions by narrow-minded Christians, especially if they live in the Bible belt. Religious tolerance is still in its infancy where witchcraft is concerned. Bigotry and religious biases are still ugly heads that rear up when witchcraft is discussed openly.

Many in today's modern society are closed minded and fearful of any group that does not fit within the puritanical, Christian standard. When we add the term witchcraft as an ingredient, suddenly the Christian churches feel it is their right to be the judge, jury and executioner and expunge the perceived wickedness. That is exactly what took place throughout Europe, spreading over to America during the Salem

Witch Trials. What a horrifying time to live, not knowing if your neighbor was going to accuse you of witchcraft simply because he or she disliked you or because he or she woke up one morning with a chip on their shoulder.

Instead of practicing love and compassion, knowing that God forgives the sinner and leaving the judgement up to the ultimate Judge, the militant religious fanatics took charge. Thus, fear and bondage reigned, resulting in the old medieval practices of torturing and burning of anyone thought to be a witch or anyone who dared to disagree with the Church. In a society that came to America from England to escape religious intolerance, the Salem religious leaders showed no love or compassion to their own denomination members who were accused of witchcraft. Their fear and superstition were like a disease that rapidly infected the entire community. It was another dark day for Christianity.

Wicca is so varied that practitioners pick and choose the rituals they perform in their covens. A coven being composed of a small group of like-minded individuals, almost like a small congregation in a community church. There are no set rules, and everyone does it differently. Many find happiness and fulfillment in their acceptance of the Wicca faith. The Wiccan religion is recognized as a legal religion. In 1986 the Federal Appeals court fourth circuit Judge J. Butzner, affirmed the ruling in *Dettmer vs. Landon* (799F.ed 929). The affirmation clearly set Wicca as a religion under the protection of constitutional rights. The Federal Courts said that Witchcraft is a legitimate religion and falls within a recognizable religious category. Legally, Wicca is accepted, but socially, Wicca is still feared by the Christian sects who continually label Wiccan practice as demonic and evil and a bane on society.

Mrs. Sue Sereno has researched and studied the Occult for more than thirty years. Mrs. Sereno said:

> *"Can you imagine calling on your God only when you are in need? Can you imagine prayers working when you demand? Can you imagine trying to bargain? Can you imagine threatening? Do you wonder*

why it doesn't work? Prayer is a daily assignment. Try sharing the good, the bad and the everyday happenings with your God. One needs to align their being into a prayer attitude that is practiced daily."

"Some people are frightened by Wicca. Why, you ask? Because it works. Wiccan's are very nice people who pray daily and though some prayers are accompanied by ritual, they are heard prayers. To address the power of prayer by Wiccans is to say it is an effective way of uniting with the God/Goddess. The Wiccan Rede says that you can do anything as long as it will bring harm to no one. To me, that is a wonderful philosophy to live by."

"There is an influx of people turning to Wicca and other alternative religions. I think it is because they are intimidated by the loud, narrow mindedness of some faiths. I can't imagine burning in Hell for not ascribing to a particular faith that pressures and threatens. And, don't forget the tithing. We were once sent tithing envelopes by a church before we were even accepted as members. People are just ready for something soothing and calm. Wicca is one of those old earth religions that puts no demands on you except to respect your fellow man and the earth we share."

"Though lots of witches practice solitary, it is thought for healing or to better affect change that it be done in numbers. This was evidenced once with a friend of mine who was diagnosed with an ovarian mass. A small group stood together in prayer and sent out energies as a unit into the Cosmos. Two weeks later, the lady was rechecked and the mass was gone. Did they heal her? I don't know, but I do know that prayer is a powerful thing. So, work your magic and don't forget prayer."

Wiccans honor the Winter Solstice or Yule as a celebration of the cycle of nature and a reaffirmation of the continuation of life. Yule is the time of greatest darkness and the longest night of the year. The Winter Solstice had been associated with the birth of a "Divine King" long before the rise of Christianity. This belief may be the psychology behind the date being chosen by the Early Church so as to associate the coming of a Divine King myth with their own beliefs of a "Divine Savior." Since the Sun is considered to represent the Male Divinity in many pagan traditions, this time is celebrated as the "return of the Sun God" where He is reborn of the Goddess. Many of the ancient cultures built their greatest architectures, such as tombs, temples, cairns and sacred observatories, so that they aligned with the solstices and equinoxes. A good example of one of these ancient sites is at Stonehenge which is aligned to both the Summer and the Winter Solstices, both indicating a change of the season.

We currently celebrate the Winter Solstice on December 21st, but anciently it was celebrated on December 25th. The Winter Solstice plays an important role in many cultures. For example, in central Tennessee, ancient Native people, constructed the Old Stone Fort so that the entrance way into the sacred ceremonial site became aligned with the North Star on the date of the Winter Solstice. Their ceremonial site was constructed over two thousand years ago and marked the beginning of Winter. It is very interesting that the Winter Solstice was even understood two thousand years ago because in our modern society, most men and women do not understand the significance to this date. We have moved from an agriculture-based society to a technologically orientated society, omitting the knowledge of planting cycles for crops as was followed and celebrated in more ancient times. The true meaning of the Summer and Winter Solstice have been lost to modern man.

We discovered that the Wicca movement was growing stronger and was becoming more popular as many were converting from Christianity to Wicca. We decided to ask a Wicca practitioner, Dr. Chanda Wright why she chose the nature-based Wicca over Christianity.

I was raised in a Lutheran home and my father was a choir director at the church. I loved church but at a very young age started to read about other faiths and go to other churches including those thought odd by my Lutheran peers, Indian, Jewish and Greek churches. Later on I dabbled in the occult and then studied ancient religions and Catholicism. It seemed to me that is was silly to have so many "religious" people calling that entity which for which simplicities sake, we will herein refer to as God, by so many different names. But worse was that one group thought another was doing it 'wrong' and their way was the only way.

It seemed to me in my studies that God loved everyone no matter how they talked to Him and was purely love, benevolence and kindness.

In my later years I found that the religions of nature seemed very natural indeed to me. In fact, I could cast spells that were good and powerful and it also seemed more sensible that my idea of God would be a "goddess" if you will. I studied Druids and Wiccan and one day read the definition of a 'natural witch.' It is and was then-me to a tee! I still think that practice of love of mother earth, nature and God is the best way, harm no one and do no evil of any sort to others! That idea did not seem to be practiced by the "religious nuts" or modern "Christians." I did not really choose it over Christianity, but developed into Wicca as I learned and grew up. I found that a lot of Christians and non-Christians are worse than skeptics and really not open to anything that they did not think of or write, in fact calling other ways evil and demonic. Who can say that Buddhism is wrong or Krishna is not a God?

It is not often that we get to meet someone whose ancestors were Gypsies from Romania, but we were led to such a person in the Southwest desert. We met Donald Swain, Circle of the Burning Sands, who was raised as a natural witch. His mother and her mother before her were hereditary witches. We asked him to share his view of life coming from a long line of witches. Donald Swain shared the following with us:

The "old religion" is the only religion I have ever known. I came from generations of those who practiced "the old ways". My ancestors were those of the Gypsies descending from Romania on my Mother's side, my Father was of Scottish descent. My whole life I had been worshiping the Crone and the Great Horned God. I had called upon the powers of the moon for help and wisdom, I had called upon the powers of the elements, Earth, Air, Water and Fire to give me strength for my magick.

We asked Mr. Swain to give us some examples of how he views life according to his pagan belief. He gave us the following examples:

If you pick an orange from a tree, you may walk away. If I pick an orange from a tree, I will stop and give thanks to the great tree for the nourishment. Better that I wait for the oranges to drop from the tree then they are offered to me and is much sweeter the taste.

I pass an animal that has been hit on the road, I ask the Goddess to allow a smooth crossover. Everything happens for a purpose. What purpose could an animal being hit on the road have? The driver who hit the animal will slow down, it's instinct, maybe by slowing down a collision was avoided up the road.

We find the examples of Donald Swain to be similar to the examples given to us by Dave Weaver who follows the Red Road. It is interesting to note that both men expressed the importance of giving thanks to their respective deity for what they have received. Unlike the repetitious Christian prayers uttered before partaking of meals, the followers of pagan faiths offers their prayers from the heart and spring forth spontaneously. It is this difference between structured prayer and spontaneous prayer that denotes another subtle aspect of the nature based religions.

In our next chapter we will examine the greatest of all, Book of Shadows, preserved in the British Museum in the form of seven codices. This famous work is known as the greatest Book of Shadows, the Key of Solomon.

The Key of Solomon

King David initiated the building of a temple in Jerusalem, which was regarded as a place in which ancient wisdom and symbolism would be reposited and preserved. It wasn't until after the King's death that his son, Solomon completed the project. He appointed Hiram, a skilled craftsman and master mason, as the chief architect. It took a period of seven years before the temple was completed after which he died a very violent and mysterious death. The Freemasons claim that Hiram was their Master who started the Freemasons.

Solomon played a major role in the occult as we know it. During the Middle Ages he gained a reputation of being a magician who had knowledge to raise elemental spirits. He also was seen as a powerful magus, healer and exorcist. The Key of Solomon is a magical text that is accredited to his authorship. Generally, the born again Christians view Solomon as being a worshiper of the devil who led the Israelites away from the true God. Yet Solomon is quoted as saying:

> "God gave me true knowledge of things as they are; an understanding of the structure of the world and the way in which the elements work, the beginning and the end of eras and what lies between, the cycles of the year and the constellations, the thoughts of men, the power of spirits, the virtues of roots, I learnt it all, secret and manifest."

Some considered Solomon's reputation of occult power and magical attributes, suggesting that he also participated in Goddess worship. He was known to have converted to paganism, worshiping strange gods. He had married foreign princesses who had introduced him to their own religious practices. It is even speculated that the Queen of Sheba introduced the King to the occult doctrines of her own land, bringing expensive gifts and her own priests to indoctrinate Solomon into the mysteries of pagan religion. With extensive communications between King Hiram and Solomon that included riddles in which Solomon had to solve, that secret information was being transmitted in code. The theory being that Solomon was a student of Hiram Abiff, learning the mysteries of the goddess Ishtar or Astarte and her ascent into the underworld, or what we refer to as Hell.

Occult tradition purports that Hiram Abiff was a member of the secret society, Dionysian Artificers that first appeared around the time of BC 1000 during the time the temple was being built in Jerusalem. They settled in Israel, founding the Cassidens, a guild of craftsmen who were skilled in the repair of old buildings. This new sect was the beginning foundation of the Essenes, a mystical Jewish group. The fame of the Essenes came with the discovery of the Dead Sea Scrolls. Occult tradition tells us that Jesus of Nazareth was Essene and there is a connection between the Essenes and the secret society, the Knights of Templar. This group, dedicated to helping the poor had incorporated the use of secret signals, handshakes and signs so as to recognize each other.

It has been suggested that the original temple was used, for 200 of the 370-year history, for Goddess worship. During that time it wasn't an unusual practice to worship gods and goddesses. In fact until the onset of Christianity, spiritual beliefs were not monotheistic, but included both male and female entities, each having their own respective place in worship.

The fact remains that the temple was built in pagan fashion, a temple to a Goddess, Isis, Ishtar or Astarte and was designed as symbols of her body, reflected in the sacred architecture. The two pillars in front of Solomon's temple resemble Canaanite fertility symbols. There are similarities between these pillars and the monoliths used by Lamech to preserve ancient knowledge, carved as symbols on their surfaces. They have been identified as masculine and feminine symbols by which the Universe came into being, also as depicted on the Tree of Life.

In Masonry, God is referred to as the Great Architect of the Universe, relating the importance of geometry in the building of sacred places based on the Hermetic precept of 'As above...so below.' This is an indication of the ancient philosophy that this plane of existence is the mirror image of the spiritual realm.

We know very little about how he acquired his magical talents, but tradition has it that it is all recorded in his famous Book of Shadows called, *The Key of Solomon*. This Book of Shadows is one of the most sought after books in Witchcraft. The only surviving manuscripts of this Book of Shadow, is found in the British Museum. If other copies existed, they have been lost to antiquity. Unless one was gifted in the language of Latin, the seven codices of the Key of Solomon would still remain under lock and key in the British Museum. However, we are fortunate as at the close of the eighteenth century, a scholar and fellow magician translated the seven codices into English.

The Keys of Solomon the King was translated and edited into English and published late in 1889 by S. Liddell MacGregor Mathers, considered to be one of the pre-eminent magicians of his time. The genesis and repository of Qabbalistical Magic, and the origin of much of the Ceremonial Magic of mediaeval time is said to be found in the 'Key'. *The Keys of Solomon* is held with the same veneration as orthodox Christians hold for the legendary Ark of the Covenant supposedly hidden in a remote monastery in Ethiopia, the famed Holy Grail, conceivably the cup that Jesus drank from at the Last Supper or the Holy Spear of Longinius, the alleged spear used by the Roman soldier who thrust it into the side of Jesus while he was on the Cross. These orthodox Christian holy relics are esteemed as sacred and hallowed in the same manner as the Key of Solomon is venerated as the sacred Book of Shadows.

The authorship of the 'Key' is assigned to King Solomon more by tradition then by any other source. The Jewish historian, Josephus does mention the magical works attributed to King Solomon and yet King Solomon's magical skills are frequently mentioned in the Arabian

Nights. King Solomon was regarded as the greatest wizard of his time and claimed to have received his knowledge inspired by the wise teachings of an Angel sent from God.

Near the time of his death, Solomon left to his son, Roboam, a Testament which contained all the wisdom he had possessed prior to his death. The Rabbins who cultivated this knowledge called this Testament, the Clavicle or Key of Solomon which they caused to be engraved on pieces of tree bark, while the Pentacles were inscribed in Hebrew letters on plates of copper. This Testament was in ancient times translated from Hebrew into the Latin language by Rabbi Abognazar. The oldest manuscript in the King Solomon Collection in the British Museum, dates back to about the middle of the sixteenth century and is in Latin.

The secrets found in the Key of Solomon reveal the profoundest mysteries of ancient Occult Science written by King Solomon and are hidden within this Key of Secrets. When the Sepulchre containing the body of King Solomon was unearthed, an ivory casket was discovered inside, which contained the Key of Secrets. When: Babylonian Philosophers attempted to read the Key of Secrets, none could understand it due to the obscurity of the words, occult arrangement and the hidden character of the meaning and knowledge. Therefore, it is plain that the secrets lay in an occult arrangement and in the words associated with the pentacles. After careful reading of this book many times, we would like to suggest that the secret of understanding hidden Occult Science spoken about within the Key of Solomon, lies in understanding the *Magic Dimensions.*

Let us start with some important concepts presented in the Introduction to *The Keys of Solomon the King.* King Solomon speaks of concealing all secrets of magical arts in this Key when he said the following:

> *"And I composed a certain work wherein I rehearsed the secret of secrets, in which I have preserved them hidden, and I have also therein concealed all secrets whatsoever of magical arts of any master; any secret*

or experiments, namely, of those sciences which is in any way worth being accomplished. Also I have written them in this Key, so that like a key openeth a treasure-house, so this Key alone may open the knowledge and understanding of magical arts and sciences."

In another part of the Introduction, we are told about the nature of different kinds of spirits. This is the beginning of understanding that everything has a spirit. The understanding that spirits control or have force over the various aspects of our planet may be hard for some to understand. Consider the following comments from the Introduction:

"There are different kinds of Spirits, according to the things over which they preside…there are master. And also (spirits) in the Elements as well as in the Heavens, there are some in the Fiery Regions, others in the Air, others in the Water, and others upon the Earth, which call all render service to that man who shall have the good fortune to understand their nature, and to know how to attract them."

The modern day pagan or witch still calls upon the spirits of the four powers, Fire, Air, Water and Earth when conducting ceremonies. This concept of spirits who have dominion over Fire, Air, Water and Earth may have originated with the teachings of the great Wizard and Magician, King Solomon. The source of witchcraft is lost in the pages of antiquity, as no solid evidence has been found that documents the beginnings of the Craft.

King Solomon believed that God has destined to each of us a spirit, which watches over us and takes care of our preservation. In modern times, we call this entity, a Guardian Spirit or Guardian Angel. In former days, King Solomon called this spirit, Genii. We recall the tales of the Genie and the bottle from the Arabian Nights. Perhaps the Genii is not so far fetched as today many believe in Guardian Angels. Our terminology has changed, but the concept still remains alive today.

The Works of Solomon is divided into two books. In the first book there are guidelines for experiments, operations and the spirits themselves. The second book teaches about magical art and how to cast the spells. It is interesting to note that King Solomon refers to the Master of the Art as an Exorcist, or Practitioner of Magic. King Solomon considered this form of magic as an Occult Science, or hidden science. It is hard for us in the twenty-first century to comprehend the existence of Occult Sciences, but during the time period of King Solomon, the belief in magic was strong and unlike today, it was practiced and it did work. Today we can use magical words in the form of prayers to heal a sick person which is then called a miracle. It seems that miracles are acceptable to the general public, yet if we replace the term miracle with the word, magic, this word draws stares and snickers.

The Keys of Solomon speak much about conjuring spirits when specific knowledge is desired. These conjured spirits might be compared to the Greek mythological Gods, such as Neptune pictured with his trident standing guard over the oceans. If Sailors drown from an angry storm at sea, the God Neptune is not considered demonic or evil. He is simply Neptune and depending on his whims, the sea may be calm or it may be angry. This is similar to how King Solomon describes his conjured spirits. The "evil" spirits are conjured as mild, harmless and handsome spirits and when they have imparted their teachings, they are bid to depart without causing harm to anyone. King Solomon worked with spirits of all kinds, each according to the knowledge they possessed.

The spirits so conjured are used as a source of knowledge and are not compelled to do harm to others. It appears that conjuring evil spirits are not against the Hebrew law if one does not use these evil spirits for evil purposes. One must focus on the knowledge itself that is gained rather then viewing the source of that knowledge. The messengers who deliver the message are not condemned. This practice of accepting knowledge or truth without evaluating the messenger has been lost over the years. Today we shoot the messenger if we don't like the message. Perhaps therein lies one of the keys to understanding Occult Science.

Solomon warns his son, Roboam about the 'Key' and how it is to be used. Consider the following from *The Key of Solomon the King*, Book 1, chapter VIII:

> *"Furthermore thou shall vanquish all adversities, and shalt be cherished and loved by the Angels and Spirits, provided that thou hast made their characters and that thou hast them upon thee; I assure thee that this is the true way to succeed with ease in all thine operations, for being fortified with a Divine Name, and the Letters, Characters, and Sigils, (signs) applicable unto the operation, thou shall discover with what supernatural exactitude and very great promptitude, both Terrestrial and Celestial things will be obedient unto thee. But all this will only be true, when accompanied by the Pentacles which hereinafter follow, seeing the Seals, Characters, and Divine Names, serve only to fortify the work, to preserve from unforeseen accidents, and to attract the familiarity of the Angels and Spirits;"*

In order to understand the Key of Solomon, one must understand the world view held by most people regarding the magical arts. Magic was once, widely accepted by the people of the land. Sorcerers were common and King Solomon was considered the most powerful. He could conjure up spirits who would teach him the mysteries of God. In that time, the Old Testament religion was a way of life, unlike today where modern religion is worn on the sleeve to be seen of men. King Solomon was a Hebrew who understood the sacred significance of the Hebrew symbols. All of his prayers and conjurations involved calling upon the holy names of God and Angels and of writing their sacred names in Hebrew. Westerners may have problems comprehending the special place that Hebrew Letters play in the overall world view of magic.

The Book of The Sacred Magic of Abramelin the Mage taught that Michael, Gabriel, Raphael, and the others are not names but titles. Perhaps the most difficult aspect to overcome in understanding the Key of Solomon is removing the contamination spread by the Christian sects. Christianity teaches concepts that are diametrically opposed in the

Hebrew faith. Christianity teaches a narrow and restrictive version of religion that prevents the secrets of the Key of Solomon from being understood and comprehended. There appear to be psychological conflicts between Christianity and the older Hebrew Qabbalistical Magic. Anyone who is not of Hebrew lineage would not understand the language and symbols employed and thus would not be able to achieve the same results.

In order to gain a better understanding about how the ancient text employs the term demons or devils, we again refer to the magic book translated by S. Liddell MacGregor Mathers. This manuscript was translated from the original Hebrew into French and then translated into English by Mathers. The important insight gained from this, the A.D. 1458 manuscript known as *The Book of the Sacred Magic of Abramelin the* Mage, was how demons or devils were viewed in the fifteenth century. Mathers said, "The word 'Demon' is evidently employed in this work almost as a synonym of Devil; but, as most educated people are aware, it is derived from the Greek 'Daimon,' which anciently simply meant any Spirit, good or bad." Consider the impact of this statement. Demon, by definition, connotes any Spirit, good or bad! If we apply the same content to people today, some are good and some are bad. We can still interface with people who are bad, we simply have to set the parameters that one needs to function within. Important concepts have been lost, such as the example above. In five centuries, we have taken the term demon and gone from Spirits, good or bad to a Spirit that is very evil.

King Solomon's use of ceremonial magical arts, such as the magic circle, the magical sword, the staff, the magical wand, censer and incense that helped to establish the frame of mind necessary to conjure the spell. His description of the nine-foot circle within a circle suggests that those in Wicca and Witchcraft are employing a form of the sacred circle. As in any ancient art, many valuable components have been lost in antiquity. Imagine what someone would do if they understood the secrets contained in the Book of Shadows, one of the greatest books ever to be written by the hand of man!

How does the Key of Solomon relate to the *Magic Dimensions*? The relationship becomes clear when one understands the intensity required to perform the magic taught by King Solomon. One has to view ceremonial magic art as a way of establishing a mind set that is focused on the purpose of the ceremony. While many of the magical spells appear to operate outside science, we must be cautious so as not to turn a blind eye simply because we do not understand the science behind the event. The concept of quantum mechanics is veiled in mystery and weirdness, even to the prophets of science whose profession is to delve into the quantum physics. It is no wonder that ordinary folks like us can find this concept difficult at best and frustrating at worst.

After careful reading of the Key of Solomon my conclusion is that King Solomon applied what we are calling the Language of Prayer, but cloaked in the mysticism of Hebrew Qabbalistical Magic. We do know that the pentacle symbol Solomon used on his Temple was later adopted by the Jewish faith as their religious symbol, the Star of David. Do not be alarmed or frightened by the term pentacle as it simply means a symbol that can be worn or displayed, similar to the Christian Cross or the patron saints medallions carried by members of the Catholic Church.

Christianity

Disraeli said, "The world is governed by very different personages from what is imagined by those who are not behind the scenes." This statement has more truth in it than most will comprehend. What occurs behind the scene is more important than what is presented on stage for the world to view. The on-stage production is orchestrated for a specific effect achieved by those performing. The performers follow the script given to them by those behind the scene who pull the strings on how the performance is presented.

Magic works if you believe it will work, but for Christians the concept of magic is clouded with trepidation and fear because all magic is considered black magic which translates into demonic intervention and a lost of salvation for any faithful member who delves into this forbidden art. The outrage expressed by Christians who gathered for a book burning of the Harry Potter's series of books is reflective of their attitudes toward magic. It would not be fair to ignore a discussion on the origin of this sect who felt compelled to burn books on magic and murder innocent people as it did during the Salem Witch Trials of 1692, all in the name of God. Why does these sects have such a caustic outlook toward magic can only be understood by pealing away the protective masks and examining the true nature of this book burning sect.

Christianity and pagan theology are not separate and distinct, but are interwoven in a convoluted labyrinth that ecclestical leaders would prefer remain buried and forgotten. Once the skeletons fall from the closet, the truth becomes apparent. While Christianity today condemns magical rituals, historical documents reveal a different story. According to the book *Ancient Christian Magic: Coptic Texts of Ritual Power* by Marvin Meyer and Richard Smith, the Coptic Orthodox

Church (Egyptian Christians) practiced Christian Magic rituals for over eleven hundred years, from AD 100 to about AD 1200. The ancient Christian Magic included spells, charms and amulets, used in their rituals. Coptic text records Jesus conducting magical rituals during baptismal ceremonies. Magic was a part of the Christian religion for over a thousand years, yet today that same magic is condemned and rejected by the Church. Let us explore the transition of this religion called Christianity.

Miracles is the product of believing in Christianity, at least according to doctrinal teachings of the modern day Christians. Miracles are suppose to be the handiwork of God to the faithful when requested by humble prayer. Transformation are transcendental and are accorded miraculous status by Christians who claim the miracle came through the grace of God. How these transformations occur is not understood nor why a transformation fails to materialize when it is petitioned to God. If we are to understand the physics of miracles, we must understand the origins of Christianity. The study of Christianity is a study in the tangled web of deception, greed, control, power, and economic supremacy. When we speak of the early Church, we refer to the Gnostic Christian Church, the Coptic Orthodox Church and the Romanized Christian Church which coexisted at the same time. This does not suggest for a minute that there existed mutual harmony between these Christian sects. Just the opposite existed, contention and a constant struggle by each sect to achieve power and position. The Romanized Christians won out and by aligning with the State, it became the most powerful institution in the land, thereby crushing all other contenders for the title.

At first glance, one might assume that Christianity was a God inspired religion that provided the path for redemption and salvation. However, when examined more closely, the history is filled with the follies of men seeking position and power. This is a most shocking revelation, having been practicing Christians for most of our adult lives. We were surprised and appalled. The history was not as we had been taught by our Sunday School teachers, but involved a deep tangled web of deception and greed. The background of the Christian church was not one of prophets and revelations where God talks to man, but rather where man talks to man. The history is not simply cut and dry as we tend to believe, but rather years and years of discussion, decision making and deception based upon control of the people and economic conditions of the time.

The historical Christian Church has acquired most of their "inspired" teachings, not from a divine source, but from other pagan religions. Recent archeological findings suggest that previous validation of Biblical history may be in error and that some of the Biblical accounts may be mythological, as no verifiable findings substantiate the events having occurred in the time frame specified in the Bible. Scholars are now stepping forth and suggesting that their findings may not have verified the historic data recorded in the Bible. Some scholars are even suggesting that some of the historic data is fiction. Now lets examine how the role of Christianity was influenced by pagan magic.

If we said that Christianity was a byproduct of many pagan religions, we would anger and cause outrage among Christians. Christians fears the word pagan or the associated witchcraft because they have been indoctrinated into the belief that the Christian Church represents good and the pagan beliefs and witchcraft represent evil. This duality is essential in maintaining control over Church members. The members must feel that the Church is their only defense against evil and the only doorway to salvation. The reason we point out the historical background is because pagan practices have a stigma associated with them due to the negative ramifications depicted by the Church. The Church proclaims that if one delves into paganism or anything associated with the darkness of the unknown, they risk their own eternal salvation. Helen Ellerbe, author of *The Dark Side of Christian History*, said:

> *"The Reformation did not convert the people of Europe to orthodox Christianity through preaching and catechisms alone. It was the 300-*

year period of witch-hunting from the fifteenth to eighteenth century that ensured the European abandonment of the belief in magic."

The Church is a man-made institution, a legal not-for-profit corporation that seeks out profit, power and control. Examine the upper echelons of any main stream Christian Church and one would discover a vast financial network revolving around a multibillion dollar industry. For example, the Mormon Church has such a vast international financial web that even their financial audits are not released to the members. The Church Auditors simply say that the records have been examined and conform to standard acceptable accounting practices. Amazing since the audits are completed by Mormon Accountants and the results are kept secret from the membership at large, though it is the membership that contributes to these holdings.

The Mormon Church (Church of Jesus Christ of Latter Day Saints or LDS) is one of the wealthiest religious corporations, second perhaps only to the Vatican, yet it still asks for more money from their members in the form of tithing and "Fast Offerings." Why? The original justification given for having tithing was to support the Mormon Church during it early days of financial insolvency, but that reason is no longer valid, yet the Church continues to rake in the donations. Where do all the hundreds of millions of dollars go today? Of all that is collected, a very small portion is allotted to new buildings, building maintenance and welfare programs. A vast treasure has been accumulated, all under ownership of the President of the Church who holds title to all property and assets within the Church. Yes, all monies collected by local units each week must be deposited in the local bank accounts of this Salt Lake City based Church. The money flows back to the Mother Church each Monday as the deposits are processed.

The financial contributions of each member are tracked by the Church and if ten percent of the individual's income is not paid in tithing and about two percent paid to the Fast Offering, then the special Temple Recommend that allows entrance into the Mormon Temples are denied the individual. The individual is also denied the ability to hold key positions within the local Church unit. If tithing is not paid, Mormons cannot enter into the highest level of their Celestial Kingdom, or Heaven. Hence, for Mormons, salvation is predicated on the donation of money to the Church!

What is salvation? This concept originated with the early Church as a psychological tool to maintain absolute control over others. When we speak of salvation, it is used in reference to eternal existence after our mortal death. Since there is no documentation of someone being physically dead, buried and coming back to reveal the truth of this concept, the concept must be considered a theory, void of proof. This is not to dismiss the documentation of NDE, or Near Death Experience, which is just as it says, Near Death. The NDE is still controversial, some scientist claiming the experience is related to chemical reactions within the brain while others suggest the soul or spirit has left the body, but not abandoned the body. The NDE experiences suggest that our existence is not determined by salvation granted by a religious body, but is an individual experience.

The religious community boldly declares that salvation is a fact because the proof is found in the Bible. This is the same Bible that is a translation of a translation, the same Bible that was created with sixty-six books in AD 325, but what about other 'religious' text that existed at this time? The Gnostic and Coptic texts were burned to eliminate competition with the 'Constantine Approved' version of Christianity.

In order for Constantine to unify the Roman Christian empire, he had to eliminate all contenders, such as Gnostic Christians and Coptic Christians, by destroying all knowledge about them. In support of this unification, the Christians under Bishop Theophilius, burned down the world's greatest library of human knowledge, at Alexandria. The Church banned education on the basis that the 'spread of knowledge' could only serve to encourage heresy. Consequently, the Church eliminated education so its members would remain ignorant and dependent on the Church for its source of information and knowledge about God.

Probably the most significant event for the Church took place in Turkey on 20 May AD 325. This was the Council of Nicaea, the results of the Emperor Constantine's decision to take charge of his fragmented empire. At that time Rome was no longer the power it had once been. The Emperor could no longer hold control over his subjects by force or financial reward, but he could control them if he inserted himself into the spiritual beliefs of his subjects. Constantine was a follower of the Sol Invictus sun god cult, but history will note him as the legitimizer of Christianity.

Thus, Emperor Constantine's beliefs and practices had to be absorbed into the collection of books that would become known as the Bible. The Counsel members were careful to not offend the Emperor by removing any text that was not acceptable to the Emperor. Many changes were also made in how the Church viewed doctrinal issues of their day. One very good example of how major changes to common practice were decided upon, would be the many interesting doctrines that were discussed and resolved by the Council of Nicaea. One of the most debated topics was the question of the divinity of Jesus.

Researchers, Christopher Knight and Robert Lomas, authors of *The Second Messiah*, stated that one of the heated debates that took place in the Council of Nicaea regarded the vote on whether or not Jesus was a deity. Apparently this heated debate continued all day and wasn't resolved until the close of the day. The Council had agreed to consider the Jewish leader a god. This implies that for over three hundred and twenty-five years the Christian Church considered Jesus as a man and not a god. This would be consistent with the Gnostic Christian text that stated Jesus was a man, not a god. The divinity of Jesus didn't become doctrine until the fourth century. Even the Jewish people who were contemporaries with Jesus did not accept him as being divine. According to Knight and Lomas, this was the beginning of the Dark Ages.

Many changes were made in how the Church viewed holidays. For example, Constantine changed the time of the Easter celebration from

Friday, Saturday or Sunday to Easter being celebrated on the first Sunday after the first full moon, on or after the vernal equinox. In Christianity Easter is one of the most sacred of holy days. It is a day that commemorates the miracle of faith when Christ was risen from the grave, so why didn't the Christian Church use the date of the actual resurrection instead of adopting the pagan holiday used by non-Christians? Other Gnostic Christians suggested the resurrection was a spiritual resurrection and not a literal resurrection which would seem to suggest why the Church did not use the original date prior to 20 May AD 325.

Today, Christmas is a sacred Christian holiday, but why was December 25th chosen for the celebration of Christ's birth? There is no date given for the event in the Bible, but Biblical scholars agree, Jesus was born in September or October rather than during the colder Winter months. Clues to this are given in the Bible where St. Luke tells of shepherds in the fields watching over their flocks by night. The fact is that shepherds guarded the flocks' day and night but only during the lambing time which was in the Spring and Fall. During the Winter months, animals were kept in corrals and were left unwatched.

Birthdays were not celebrated and until the fourth century, the birth of Christ was down played more than acknowledged. The Church had actually announced that it was sinful to consider recognizing Christ's birth as he was not royalty. It was on December 25th that the pagan Romans celebrated the birth of the sun god, Mithras. Mithraism was such a popular religion that it was declared as the official state religion by the year AD 274.

Mithra was born of a virgin in a stable on 25 December around BC 600. His resurrection was celebrated at Easter. Mithraism is a Syrian offshoot of the more ancient Persian cult of Zoroaster. Its doctrines included baptism, a sacramental meal, belief in immortality, a messiah god who died and rose again to act as a mediator between man and god, a resurrection, a last judgement and heaven and hell. The cult seriously threatened the continued existence of Christianity in the early

3rd century so the Church fathers needed to make a decision. It was decided the Church would have a December holiday too and to give converts the chance to celebrate as they always had, the Church recognized Christ's birth. As competition to the festivities of the sun worshipers the Church chose, December 25th. The fact that Mithraism was practiced for six hundred years before the birth of Christianity did not stop the Church from declaring that Mithraism was the counterfeit religion and Christianity was the true religion.

The Roman's loved celebrations and feasts and actually had over 100 days a year set aside for celebrating. The more holidays, the happier they were. There was another side to the partying and celebrating though. There was and is a social psychology behind group celebrations, which includes the unifying and strengthening of beliefs, solidarity in identity and reinforcing the objectives and goals held by people. It was not only a time of joyous celebration, but a time of those with like beliefs, strengthening themselves. The social implications are very important, although people rarely think about anything outside of the celebrating. Christmas in the western world became set in 337 A.D., when Constantine, Emperor of Rome was baptized. For the first time in history the Church and the Crown were united. It was 313 A.D. when Christianity reigned as the official state religion in Rome. In 354 A.D. it was Bishop Liberius of Rome who proclaimed the importance of celebrating not only Christ's death, but also his birth.

Christmas and Easter are two significant holidays celebrated today by Christians as the birth and resurrection of their Savior. These two important dates in Christendom are celebrated on dates assimilated from pagan holidays that predated Christianity. Easter or the time of the resurrection is very common among the agricultural-based cultures. This is a time designated for fertility rites which originated in or around the Spring Solstice, for the purpose of obtaining fertile crops and abundance of harvest. It is the Springtime when new plant and animal life spring forth, having been dormant through the winter months. The rebirth of new life begins in the Spring and corresponds to the resurrection, or the rebirth of Jesus. The Norsemen celebrated the rebirth by having their god tied with outstretched arms to a tree, very similar to the Christian Cross. The concept behind the resurrection is not new, but has been long told in the mythology of various cultures long before the advent of Christianity. A divine Church would have no need to resort to piracy of pagan holidays, if it was truly divine.

This practice of taking from one religion and associating it with another is still continued today. For example, the Temple ceremonies of the Mormon Church, which is their holiest of rituals, were but an alteration of the Freemason or Masonic Temple ceremonies. The Mormon Joseph Smith proclaimed the Masonic ceremonies were corrupted and that the true Temple ceremony had been revealed to him by God. However, this divine revelation transpired after Joseph Smith was expelled as the head of the largest Masonic Lodge in Illinois, not before.

His lodge had expanded to the point of becoming a concern to other Lodges in surrounding areas. They feared their own members would be absorbed into the larger Masonic membership headed by Joseph Smith. They couldn't allow this to happen so they found reason to have him removed. After Smith Lodge was disbanded, Joseph Smith claimed to have a revelation that the Freemason Temple rituals were corrupted and that he was given the "true" ritual. Smith continued with conducting Temple ceremonies after being expelled from the Freemasons, but this time he conducted those ceremonies as the spiritual leader of his Church.

It is a well-known fact that the gospels were written long after the crucifixion by those who did not witness the events though written using the names of the disciples of Jesus. Early Church Councils were the deciding factor in what would be included in the New Testament and rejected the writings that did not fit within their version of the Christian faith. The orthodox view, in the New Testament, alludes to Jesus being a descendant of Solomon of the Royal House of David. Solomon was a magician who built the temple in Jerusalem for worship of a goddess. The title to royalty that Jesus followers claimed came through the linage of Joseph, but Joseph was not the father to Jesus therefore Joseph's ancestors could not be used as validation for the royal lineage.

In the heretical gospels, the Gnostics made reference to Jesus having brothers. Joseph had died before Jesus began preaching, therefore he was called the son of a widow. Gnostic beliefs stated he was an ordinary man, overshadowed by the spirit of God becoming 'kristos' or anointed one. The survival of the physical death of crucifixion, according to the Gnostics, could only be explained if the Christ force left him before the event. The Gnostic's accepted a spiritual resurrection and did not believe in a literal physical resurrection. The Gnostic followers contented that the Constantine Christians misinterpreted the text and did not comprehend what Jesus had taught. Gnostic texts suggested that there would be no Second Coming of Jesus since there was no literal resurrection. The Second Coming takes place when we accept this "Christ force" within us, but not a literal, physical coming again of Jesus.

Many theories speculate that Jesus survived the cross, was smuggled out of the country to live a full monastic life in Kashmir in the Essene community. Perhaps he was killed at Masada during the Jewish revolt or traveled to Europe to sire the future French Royal dynasty. Regardless, the Gnostics did not accept the symbol of the cross, refusing to worship an instrument of death and torture. In approximately 90% of all of the pre-Reformation churches built before the end of the 14th Century, when church building ceased for a period of time, it was found that the altars hid fertility symbols which dedicated the Christian Churches to the old pagan religion.

In Judaism, the Cabbala is a mystical system of occult teachings. The Cabbalistic teachings reveal Lilith, the she-demon of sexual desires, influenced men by erotic dreams. Lilith was revealed as the first wife to Adam, before Eve, who taught him magical enchantment. Lilith, traced back to a Sumarian goddess, depicted in the form of an owl, also represents the dark side of the Great Goddess in ancient pagan religion. The worship of fertility goddesses was once an integral part of Judaism.

The Church forbid pagan doctrines, like that of reincarnation which was condemned by the Council of Nicaea in AD 325. It was pagan temples that were transformed into Christian Churches and pagan gods that were suddenly Christian Saints. It was an impossibility to eradicate paganism fully so the next best thing was to meld already established pagan beliefs into the new Christianity.

The Gnostics, which means knowledge, believed in direct communication with God without the need for the establishment of a priesthood. Gnosticism was the time when efforts were made to blend pagan beliefs with the newer Christian doctrines. Gnosticism got its central beliefs from the writings of Zoroaster, a Persian spiritual teacher around BC 1800. Because of a vision Zoroaster broke away from the traditional teachings of Indo-Iranian beliefs and taught his own philosophies of the universe as a battleground between the forces of darkness and light being in eternal conflict. In Zoroasterism, one had to choose between one or the other. Later, the mystery cult, Mithras, was established as an offshoot of Zoroasterism. Roman soldiers were attracted to its membership. Mithra was born, a scholar god of light, in a cave surrounded by animals and shepherds at the Winter Solstice in December.

The concept of good and evil came from the Gnostic teaching that evil was the shadow image of good and both had to exist in an imperfect world. They taught that Mithras could teach humans devoted to him, how to reconcile the good and evil of their own nature. The teachings of Mithraism were absorbed into Christianity and were promoted as Christian doctrines.

Most secret societies initiated converts by the ritual of death and rebirth. Afterward, the ritual bread and wine were shared. The communion with bread and wine represented the eating of flesh and drinking of blood of the young sun god. Today the Church employs the sacraments or communion at least once a month, but today it is wafer and wine or bread and water to represent the body and blood of Christ.

In the dark days of Christianity sanctimonious clergy members traditionally taught that everything was evil, until the Church either blessed it or baptized it. Since Nature could not be baptized or blessed, it had to be cursed and cursed it was. Nature became an enemy to God and if man wanted to return to God then he had to avoid anything dealing with nature or risk losing their eternal salvation. Nature was considered absolute evil and any rituals involving nature was considered worshiping the devil.

Marshall Philyaw, a subscriber to the International Ghost Hunters Society online Newsletter, said in regard to evil and demons:

> It is interesting, isn't it, that once one becomes conscious of the possibility that there might not be any Absolute evil, suddenly it becomes fairly easy to trace the way the monsters in our fiction are justified...to trace the path of their existence all the way back to that point of departure in the story where the author has to make allowance for the fact that in order for that monster to be possible, there has to be a belief in an Absolute, conscious, black and brooding, boiling evil; an evil that is so just for the sake of being so. Take away the acceptance of that one belief, and all the phantoms of darkness kind of fade away, for they have done run out of gas. That triple_eyed, ooze infested, drooling green and hideous monstrosity from outer space holding the fair damsel in its hairy paws suddenly becomes a charade, a mockery of itself, and perhaps a rather true reflection of the very worst beast dwelling in all of us. It is a demon that cannot truly be born of nature, but could someday be born indirectly of man, either physically or mechanically, for he alone can conceive of it. Man has no natural enemies, and the only thing he fears is fear itself.

◆   ◆   ◆

Therein lies a truth so profound that it is often missed. The demons of Christianity are created to fulfill the requirements for a third party to blame for our actions. We no longer are willing to accept responsibilities for our personal actions, but need the sacrificial goat to cleanse ourselves from our weaknesses and dishonorable actions. Any deviations from the normal and we are lost to the devil, according to the strict interpretations of Christianity. The Church teaches that evil and demons are equal in power to their protagonist, their savior. The Church has placed the devil on a pedestal and gives power to him by maintaining the fear of him stealing our human soul, if we are not careful. This is analogous to the warning given to children about the dangers of the boogey man. The boogey man is just as real to children as the demon is to Christians. When we play upon the fears instilled by man made religious organizations, we can control the masses without chains. We have psychological manipulation at its best. Science fiction writers have written books for over fifty years suggesting that if one controlled the priesthood, than one could control the people.

Thus, the fear of demons intimidates and scares Christians today, just as the sanctioned acts of violence and the use of intimidation by the early Church kept many people from following after the pagan practices of their times. The power of Church and State effectively blocked the spread of magic. In the duality of any system, the church accepted magic if it was politically expedient or if the "powers that be" wanted it. The church even accepted some of the magical rituals common to the time and incorporated them into their own version with different ceremonial names.

Christian concepts of the Original Sin provided the handcuffs and leg irons necessary to incarcerate Church members with psychological issues, such as fear, guilt and shame, least they suffer the loss of everlasting redemption. This psychological bondage resembles the chain gangs of the south, where prisoners are chained together so they cannot escape. However, in this case, the binding chains are forged from psychological issues of fear, guilt and shame. Original Sin kept men and women in bondage, slaves to man made religious doctrines. If they were not good, they would not be saved. Being born as sinners, they would die sinners unless they redeemed themselves and accepted the Christian savior.

Today Christian sects use guilt and fear as bondage tools to keep their members subservient to the will of the leaders of the churches. Any deviation from the acceptable way results in threats of damnation and hell's fire. The motif of a shepherd leading his flock of sheep often is portrayed by the Church. However, using sheep as an example was a rather poor choice for icons because as any good farm boy knows, sheep are dumb animals and will follow other sheep anywhere, even over a cliff to their death. We suggest that breaking away from congregational bondage or as we see it, breaking free of the sheep mentality and aspiring to become the shepherd is what this book is all about. Truth is everywhere, but not everyone is willing to accept it. What we need is more shepherds, not more sheep being led blindly down the path.

The acceptance of religion also programmed its members into a different notion of how time is looked upon. A central tenet of the Jewish faith, inherited by both Christianity and Islam, was that of the historical process, whereby God's propose for this biosphere emerges according to a definite temporal sequence. In this system of belief, God created this biosphere at a definite moment in the past, from a different state of conditions than exist today. The theological arrangement of linear events: creation, fall, redemption, judgment, resurrection, is paralleled by what Science suggests were the sequence of physical events. The Big Bang or order out of primeval chaos, origin of the earth, origin of life from primeval soup, origin of mankind, annulment and collapse. This concept of linear time suggests the implication of the river of time which flows one way, flowing from past to future and indicating the direction of sequential events.

However, this tenet of linear flow was not inherited by those who followed the pagan beliefs and therefore, they symbolically represent their ceremonies in circles, or as science would suggest, cyclic representations. The symbol of the circle also suggests that there is no beginning and no end, that all are interconnected within the circle. Christianity can only operate on a linear sequence of events. Thus, the religion condemns the concept of being interconnected with others while promoting their linear version of past, present and future with no connection between each time frame. The cyclic sequence lies outside of their understanding and comprehension. Thus, for Christianity, the concept of magic is foreign to their belief system since magic is not based on linear movement of time, but on cyclic or recurring cycles, much like the recurring lunar cycles or like tidal movement. This duality of cyclic versus linear provided the foundations that each set of beliefs was assimilated upon.

The natural cycles of nature as circles within circles is in contrast to the straight or linear progression of creation, fall, redemption, judgment to resurrection. The two philosophies have roots that are in conflict with each other. It is no wonder that Christians judges all pagan worship ceremonies as being Satanic in nature. Their judgements are not based on facts, but upon their understanding of the nature of time and the sequence of events. Their justification for condemnation lies tangled in a quagmire stemming from a belief system that followed a linear path based upon their observation of how time is treated by man. The linear path has to be narrow, restrictive and unforgiving because as a river flows in one direction it never repeats itself, thus, linear sequence does not allow for cyclic occurrences or the interconnectedness of all things.

Perhaps this is why Christianity found conflict with the Asian theology which does not accept time as being linear, but as cyclic, operating in cycles that repeat themselves. There were and are complex factors that influenced and polarized Christianity. Factors that prevented the Christian Church from accepting magic as part of its tenants. Magic operates outside the linear sequence of time and must be understood according to the cyclic notion of time.

Another conflict lies in how each religion treats their members. The Christian Churches employ some excellent psychological techniques, such as shame, guilt and fear to keep its members in alignment with accepted Church teachings. If we remove shame, guilt and fear, the Church would have no hold over anyone. No threats of damnation, no fear of losing our salvation and no shame for questioning Church doctrines. What we discovered was that we were no longer in bondage to a belief system that did not allow us to question the validity of the historical claims of the Church. The followers of nature-based religions treat each individual as being special and unique. Each person is a representation of nature and nature is considered to be divine. Each individual is considered to be interconnected to all living things and to nature itself. This is opposite to how Christianity view its members, not to mention those outside of their sect.

 According to Harry R. Moody and David Carroll book, *The Five Stages of the Soul,* the difference between a spiritual path and a religious path is that religion applies to the outer aspects of worship, ritual, doctrine, and congregational practice. Spirituality pertains to the deepest and innermost relationship with the sacred, Higher Power. We do not define what this Higher Power is because that is what this book is all about. We began our search for magic and once we found it, discovered how it is accessed and implemented into our lives. So call it magic or miracle, it's all in a name. Spirituality is an individual issue that cannot be addressed by congregational practices nor by opinions expressed from the pulpit, regardless of what robes of power are worn by the speaker. Spirituality must be experienced on a soul level, not discussed in a logical frame work. We believe that when you practice magic you will experience spirituality at its most fundamental level.

The idea that being a Christian will invoke special gifts and powers from God are without foundation. The idea that God inspired the Bible is a myth. The idea that miracles happen by the grace of God is a myth. The disciples of Christianity are taught that the Church is the vehicle through which salvation is granted and that they are saved by the grace of God alone. Their access to God is by prayers of petition which may or may not be answered. For the Christian, prayer is the gateway for change or transformation. Prayer is the gateway for transformation, but there is a protocol that must be followed to achieve desired success. Prayers of petition will fall on deaf ears, but following the proper protocols will result in successful results. In the next chapter we will discuss the history of prayers and how it has evolved. Later we will have a chapter specifically on the protocols for the Language of Prayer and how it differs from the Christian concept of prayers.

The History of Prayer

Prayer is one of the most ancient expressions of religion. It is the human act of communicating with God, gods or goddesses or with any transcendent realm. Our word, "prayer" is taken from the Anglo-Saxon 'bede' meaning bead, derived from 'bidden' that means to beg. Theologians have divided prayer into five different categories that have been around since primitive times. The purest form of prayer being the contemplation of God which could be related to the intense meditation practiced by mystics. It is a prayer of asking for nothing, but bowing down in adoration of the Creator.

The most common form of prayer is, petitions, asking God for something we desire. To Mystics, this has always been the lowest form of prayer or begging. In fact, it was St. Augustine that said, "Man is a beggar before God." When we have acknowledged ourselves to have sinned, our prayer is one of confession, at which time we seek forgiveness. When we praise the Lord for all He has done for us, we recite a prayer of praise.

A prayer of thanksgiving was one in which thanks was given for the victory over an enemy in ancient times, whereas the pilgrims gave thanks for the abundance of food on the first Thanksgiving Day in1621 at Plymouth, Massachusetts. Hebrew tradition was to give thanks to Yahweh for an abundant harvest, followed by eight days of celebrating. It was the Roman Catholics that established the ritual of saying grace before partaking in a meal.

Prayer, according to William James, is "Religions primary mode of expression." He says that religion could not exist without the concept of prayer. Prayer is the means by which we communicate with God or a higher power. St. John of Damascus said that prayer was, "Elevation to the mind of God." Prayer is a major part of every known religion, everywhere. We all pray the same though the direction and belief may differ. In Indian mysticism, prayer is considered to be as vital as breathing. To pray and be Muslim, is synonymous.

The first mention to prayer in the Bible comes early in the book of Genesis (Gen.4:26). The foundation of prayer becomes set in that man asks, God hears and maybe, just maybe, God answers. It was Jesus who said, "Whatever you ask in prayer, believe that you receive it and you will. All things are possible to him who believes." (Mark11:24; 9:23). If our prayer of petition goes unanswered, we can then tell ourselves we did not truly believe enough, we lacked devoutness, that God doesn't feel the request to be beneficial to us or that we have not prayed long enough. Early religions believed that frequent repetition of prayer increased its effectiveness.

What about bodily expression used during prayer? To join the hands together, fingers entwined and palms held together, in ancient times was a sign of submission. Yet the clasping of hands during prayer is mentioned nowhere in the Bible. It appeared in the Christian Church during the ninth century. Religious historians have linked it to the act of being shackled or bound as a prisoner. Christianity assumed the gesture to depict obedience. In Colonial America, preachers used this gesture as a method of controlling children from fidgeting during the long church services.

Bowing the head, for centuries in prayer, indicates humility. A pagan posture that stems from the earliest days of religion. Kings demanded subservience and bowing the head accomplished this. The waving of hands during prayer is a gesture to scare away evil spirits, as mentioned in the Talmud. It goes way back in history to the ancient pagan gesture for good luck. Kneeling during prayer is a sign of servitude. Kneeling was an important part of the ceremonies in the Temples of Jerusalem. When Christians adopted kneeling in their prayer postures, it became prohibited in Jewish worship. Already contention is seen as the new Christian beliefs adopt old religious practices, as their own.

In early Christianity standing was the common prayer stance, not kneeling. That changed in western churches which allowed moments for the congregation to engage in private prayer. Kneeling practices varied as Christianity splintered off into different sects, following different beliefs. Closing the eyes during prayer is to shut out distractions. This practice is ancient and found in all faiths. Activity around a person takes the focus from the prayer to other things. Prayer is meant to be fully concentrated upon, intense and for a purpose. Distraction is like the line being cut during communication with the divine.

The use of the word, Amen, after a prayer was a word of assent or agreement. The word was first used in Egypt in 2400 B.C., has pagan roots. The Egyptians worshiped 'Amun' or the hidden one, their highest deity. The Hebrews took the affirmation as their own, new meaning was give to it and passed it onto the Christians. "Amen" was used in the book of Numbers and later used twelve times in the book of Deuteronomy as assent to curses.

Early days of Christianity, congregants faced the east to pray in the direction of the rising sun. The custom is pagan and ancient when people truly worshiped the sun. High priests always had a stone altar positioned so they always faced the east. It was only a few decades ago that the Roman Catholic Church turned the altar so the priest could face the congregation, rather than the east.

Consider that 82% of Americans believe in the healing power of personal prayer. Another 73% believe prayers for someone else is a valuable aid in healing their illnesses. Another 77% believe that God intervenes at times to cure people with serious illness. Yet, 64% believe physicians should join their patients in prayer for healing, when requested. (CNN, Time Poll 1996). Research conducted at Stanford, Tufts, Harvard and Duke Universities suggests a link exists between the power of the mind and the power to heal. Studies have shown that the healing power of prayer has shown such physiological changes as reduction in blood pressure, heart rate lowering and improved immune system function. To the scientist, credit goes to a self induced physiological activity, but religious believers credit miraculous healing or events to the power of God.

In all cultures' people used some form of beaded or knotted string to help them keep track of their number of prayers. In 1119, upon the establishment of the Knights of Templar, traveling as they were, they could not attend church regularly. They were required to recite the Lord's Prayer exactly fifty-seven times a day in lieu of attendance. To keep track of these prayers, a knotted cord was used. Some cultures used the fragments of bones from a deceased loved one to keep track while the rich used gemstones or gold nuggets on which to count. Repetitive prayer was of the utmost importance and here you can understand the role of prayer beads and keeping track of the exact number of prayers prayed, as required by the church for effectiveness.

Nature and Man

The shaman and the medicine men practitioners of the Red Road view nature as the four directions, North, East, South and West. Their medicine circles are divided into four equal sections representing the four directions. The pagan magic practitioners of Witchcraft view nature as being represented by fire, water, air and earth with each element represented in a direction. It is for this reason that the powers associated with Nature have taken on an occult, or hidden quintessence. The four powers, fire, water, air and earth, are today represented as drought, floods, tornados, hurricanes, earthquakes, forest fires and volcanic eruptions and clearly demonstrate the tremendous destructive power found within nature.

Beyond the outward expression of nature, we find a less known and more subtle aspect involving nature's power that is a source for personal magical transformations. It is this less known essence that was the focal point for understanding ancient alchemy and their Philosopher's Stone. This power is energy that flows all around us and through all things. It is the energy that gives life to all living things. This energy is subtle and exists continuously within our dimension. Ancients understood this power and how to apply it in their magical rituals.

As a society, we have moved beyond the understanding and comprehension of these subtle powers found in nature because we refuse to acknowledge that there is power in nature. The influence of Christianity and its, "the natural man is an enemy to God" campaign to discredit nature those of the pagan persuasion. We have lost our ability to integrate with nature at the most basic level. We must now throw off the yoke of ignorance and work to gain understanding by opening the doors to the hidden powers found within nature.

According to the Witch's Rede, there are two mystical pillars that stand at the gate of the shrine and two are the powers of Nature, the forms and the forces divine. These two mystical pillars may represent the pillars that stood at the Temple of King Solomon. We speak of the two divine powers of Nature, the form and the force. The form is the paradigm or construct that concentrate and focus the energy found in the force.

Magic is achieved when form and force become synchronized. This orchestration of energy is not supernatural or unnatural, but is the fluid energy that is all around us, encompassing nature itself. The energies of Nature are best directed by using a magic shorthand that we call symbolism which is the language of magic and the subconscious mind. This divine power known as form, is represented through symbols that instruct the divine power of force how to direct the energy to specific ends. It is not secret, but more of forgotten magic that we speak about in this book. The methodology has been around for thousands of years, but the understanding and the application has been forgotten over time. Many ancient mystics shared this secret magic among their disciplines. Today we have Eastern religions who teach about form and force as a way to enlightenment.

Long ago, one of the most deeply reverenced magical documents was called the *Emerald Table of Hermes Trismegistus*. It is said to have been a tablet of emeralds, engraved with writing in Phoenician characters. Many theories are expressed over who discovered the tablet. Some say Apollonius of Tyana, yet others suggest the tablet was discovered by either Sarah, the wife of Abraham or by Alexander the Great, in a cave-tomb where the tablet was clutched in the fingers of the corpse Hermes Trismegistus. Hermes was the Greek god of wisdom. In Wicca, the Three Fold Rule was credited to Hermes Trismegistus so it is no wonder that he was considered the patron of magic. In Christianity, he would be the Patron Saint of Magic.

Hermes Trismegistus was supposedly a grandson of Adam, a Sage of wisdom and the builder of the pyramids. The important facet to this document is that the opening sentence, according to the Latin version circa 1200 CE, translated the opening sentence that became the groundwork for magical practice.

The translated Latin sentence reads as *"That which is above is like that which is below and that which is below is like that which is above, to achieve the wonders of the one thing."* This is the theory that man is the earthly counterpart of God: a god above so man is on earth below.

It is also a statement of the old belief that actions or events on the earth parallel the doings of the gods in heaven. The events on earth run parallel to events in heaven because both depend on the working of the same *Force*. This is the basis for the practice of astrology, that what is below is above. The alchemist of old accepted this understanding "as below so above" to explore they secrets of metal transformations which they held to be the highest level of the Philosopher's Stone.

There is a relationship between the planets and our human cycles because of the influences of the magnetic and geomagnetic fields on our human bodies. Today we can compute the magnetic fields using advanced mathematics, but we are still exploring the wonders of magnetic fields on the human body and on their effects at large. Many creatures seems to be using the magnetic fields of the earth to navigate.

Long time friend and electronics expert, Ned Stevens, suggested that the Monarch Butterfly, and the Homing Pigeon are examples of creatures in nature that have homing devices that can detect the magnetic poles of the earth. Stevens said the following:

> *"Another example that comes to mind is the Salmon that return to their birth place to spawn or when there is an earthquake in the area, animals run to and fro. I believe this occurs as the movement of the earth disrupts to magnetic lines of force, the animals loose their sense of direction. I know that the magnetic lines of force change slightly from season to season. I think the animals brains sense this as a result they start to grow their winter coats."*

The Practitioner of Magic believes that as he calls upon the full power of his will and acts accordingly, he can cause the forces of the universe, outside him to act in the same way. This is the extension of the rule of "as below, so above." Thus, working with nature is working with God because of the "as below, so above" teaching. The followers of the Red Road and the Pagan Witchcraft find no fault with Nature, they respect and give reverence to it as a part of the creation. The followers of the sects that split or splintered from the Romanized Christians abhor Nature and condemn it as an enemy of God.

Nature has never been in conflict with God or God with nature. The Christian sects teach that the natural man is an enemy to God, thus attempting to fragment man from nature. If we examine Nature, we find it has no need for a priest to intervene with God, because each person has the spark of God within them, as do all things in nature. It is this philosophical quagmire that separates those who practice paganism from those who practice the Romanized Christianity. Without the need for priest, there is no need for church structure and no place for power, greed or control to rear its ugly head.

Man is a replica of the universe and if two things are naturally associated together in the human mind, which is an image of the mind of the universe, this is evidence of a real connection between two things in the universe. This is the concept of the Sacred Hoops spoken by Black Elk, that all things are interconnected. Magic is interconnected with all of nature and all of nature is interconnected with magic. Magic is the use of the natural forces of nature to bring about needed changes.

What is this magic? We would suggest that it is nothing more than a *Force* within each of us that enables us to change future events by ceremonial procedures and application of transcendental techniques. The Chinese call this energy, *chi*, to Hindus as *prana*, to Germans as *vril*. One good, more modern representation of this force was seen in Star Wars, as Luke Skywalker was taught about the *Force*. The *Force* being a natural energy that flows all around us, stemming from our physical bodies that scientists call bio-plasmic energy. We also learned one more valuable lesson: There are no accidents, everything happens for a purpose because of the interconnectedness of all things.

Coming from the "Old Religion" we asked Donald Swain of the Circle of Burning Sands how he views nature from the pagan viewpoint:

> *As a natural witch, I was taught that every living thing and every action has a purpose. There is no such thing as circumstance. The Mother Earth guides us in our decisions. In magick we draw power from the earth and focus on our goal. For more power you would with others, all with the same goal, all drawing their power from the Mother Universe. I will draw power from the sun, the lady moon and the elements of Earth, Air, Fire and Water. The power is ours, all we have to do is accept it. All living things have power. We all come from the earth and when our lessons here are learnt, we will all return to the earth. I stand barefoot on the ground to ground myself with the earth.*

◆   ◆   ◆

From my own personal experience, I have always felt closer to God when I was in the great outdoors. At one time, I found myself in the Redwoods of Northern California and I felt serenity and peace within a wooden glen. Standing amid the tall Redwood trees, listening to the sounds of the birds and insects I was able to go deep within myself and in doing so, a veiled doorway opened to my soul. I felt at harmony with nature for the first time in my life. This was one of the few times that I felt a true reverence while standing amid the giant Redwood trees. I have never felt that kind of reverence in any church building or during services.

When we try to understand nature, we also have to understand the nature of man. If we study history, we discover that our ancestors lived in small communities that centered on and around the natural elements, the woods, glens and lakes that supported life. Unfortunately in today's society, the population is focused around major metropolitan areas for work that supports lifestyles. These cities are composed of brick, metal and glass buildings, the streets being endless miles of pavement and concrete. In the summer, the sun beats down on the paved streets relentlessly, during which reports of deaths from the heat are common among the elderly in major cities.

The denizens of these megalopolises experience the frustrations associated with work, home, family financial problems, crime or just everyday problems related to city life. For the first time in history, we have a new term that strikes fear into those commuting on the highways, called "Road Rage." Consider the drive by shootings that are so common in most major cities. The concentration of negative emotions is heightened, increasing in intensity and strength at an alarming rate. As with any build up of energy, the time comes when a control valve breaks and that energy is released. Negative emotions do not have a safety switch so it ends up being released explosively. When negativity is running high, the smallest flame can ignite the fuse. Most of us have witnessed this during our lifetimes as human nature loses it's cool.

Remember the rage people felt when terrorists attacked the Pentagon and the World Trade Center Buildings on September 11, 2001. The worst terrorist attack on American soil left thousands dead when four commercial jets, filled with passengers were hijacked for suicidal purposes, intended for mass destruction. Two airliners crashed into the twin World Trade Buildings and the third directly into the Pentagon. The fourth hijacked aircraft had passengers on board who refused to allow the hijackers to use the aircraft as a weapon of death. They fought the hijackers preventing them from carrying out their original suicidal plans, forcing the plane to crash in a field outside of Pittsburgh, PA. Osama Bin Laden became the most sought after terrorist in the world. The United States declared war on him and his terrorist organization.

The deaths and destruction that took place were done in the name of God in a religion that fundamentalists took to extremes. The beliefs became the justification for barbaric acts that took American lives so needlessly. The hijackers were young men of radical Islamic beliefs who were promised the Garden of Allah and the comfort of seventy virgin women, that would be their reward. This perverted vision was foremost in their minds as they delivered their suicidal assaults. When religion becomes more than a tenet for faith, but a justification for inflicting death onto others, then that religion has failed. This now becomes the dark side of religion that has actually filled the history books. This is the evil that men do to others while justifying their barbaric acts as God's Will! It is not demons from Hell, but the vulgar and vicious nature of man that inflicts such brutality.

Shouts of a "Second Pearl Harbor, America Attacked and War" were broadcast on almost all television channels as the media replayed the horrible video segments of the destruction of the two World Trade Buildings. We noticed while shopping in a grocery store later that day, the anger felt by one of the customers doing his shopping. He wanted revenge by nuking those responsible for this terrible crime against humanity. Our humanity was assaulted and we wanted retribution on those who cause the death and destruction. Christians were outraged that Bin Laden had called them evil and demonic. The shoes were now on the other foot for Christians because now, instead of them pointing fingers at everyone else being evil the fingers were being pointed at them and they did not like it.

People all over the United States were gathered in front of their television sets at home, in malls, in store windows, bars and restaurants watching in shock as the smoke bellowed from the World Trade Buildings. How can we as human beings not be affected by this deplorable act against humanity? How long will it take for us to heal from the instinctive anger and rage that so many felt against those who brought death and destruction to our American soil?

This whole tragedy had impacted all Americans, in many different ways. It took some time to recover from the shock, knowing so many had died, suddenly and needlessly. We started to see people pulling together, giving blood, hugging and loving each other, so thankful to be alive. I've seen the biggest, strongest men in tears saying they've never in their lives seen anything such as this. They say this is hell. How hard and horrible it would be to have to try to rescue people from all that rubble, knowing there is hardly a chance anyone else could have survived. But they are there, giving everything they have to help and people all over the world are praying for America every single day.

I just can't help but ask myself, how long after the smoke clears and life goes back to some kind of normal, will neighbors pass each other and never speak, people will go about their business and forget those around them and people overall, will just slip back into themselves, until the next tragedy happens. We should be able to love and help one another daily and not forget to say "I love you" or leave the house mad and fighting with loved ones when we don't know what might happen before returning home. We might not get another chance to apologize or to hold each other. But we forget as time passes and return to cutting remarks and hurting one another, never giving a thought to the fact that there might not be an opportunity to see those we have hurt again.

It's always so good to see folks caring for each other and pulling together for a common cause. But that's basically the only time we see that type of thing happening, after a catastrophic event where people have died needlessly and others have been injured. We must not forget that we are human beings first and foremost. We must remember the lessons learned from that terrorist attack and remain united as human beings, showing forth our love and compassion. It is not important what faith we belong to, but how we treat each other that will make the difference in the end.

It was religion, fanatical religious beliefs that caused this to happen. It isn't the religious beliefs of people that have them out there helping or giving, it's coming from their hearts, from inside of them. I've seen so much destruction done in the name of "religion" that it looks more and more to me, like it's nothing more than an excuse by which people do the things they do, be it harmful, hurtful or helpful. I've seen religious differences tear families apart. So it isn't a man's religion that makes him good or his beliefs in God, but what he does with it. Our religion should be just what we are seeing out in the "battlefield" in New York! It should be that kind of goodness that is spontaneous and freely given without expectations of something in return, like a soul conversion. We should be human beings first, regardless of our differences.

It is our nature to be positive or to be negative. We have the choice in our lives to honor one or the other and in so doing, we create either a legacy or an infamy. How we perceive, the actions of our fellow man will demonstrate our compassion or our indifference to the suffering of others. Magic is a power that can be used for positive or for negative, even the evil that men do to others. Magic is not demonic or Satanic, for man does more evil then any religious demon of theological fantasy.

With the disaster, our natures changed. Some showed love and compassion, like those who rushed in to help dig through the rubble, while others wanted immediate retribution and punishment for those responsible for the dastardly deed. The two natures of man, one filled with love and the other filled with revenge. This is reflective of the old Walt Disney cartoons where the man is having a problem making a decision and on one shoulder is an Angel in white whispering in his ear, but on the other shoulder is a little red Devil with a pitchfork also whispering in his other ear. We have the power within us, for good or for destructive acts. How we use that power determines who we are in the larger scheme of things.

There are other ways that cause man to become evil. A concentration of negative energy that becomes focused on a volatile situation that can explode at any moment is one good example. The Watts riots in Los Angeles were sparked by the negative emotions between law enforcement and the black community. When tempers are at the flare point any event can trigger negative reactions to the extreme. Major cities are breeding grounds for intense negativity. This negativity can be the fuel to feed racial unrest, religious unrest, road rage or as recently seen, terrorist attacks against Americans. Regardless of what generates the negativity, it puts people against people. Whether the terrorists of September 11th were fundamentalists who opposed all outside their faith, considering them to be demons or not, the result was mass death and destruction in the name of God. Just as the religious wars throughout our world's history.

Many have suggested relocating to small rural communities, away from the negativity of the large cities, but not everyone can afford to do so or have a desire to relocate. Those remaining in large congested cities have to work extra hard to ward off the frustration and anger that are so common on the streets and highways. In some cities there are sections directly under the control of gangs and the local police do not intervene. For many it is a war zone, constant armed conflict is the norm, drug dealers and pimps are free to ply their trade. Safety in major cities is minimal and as the population increases, the anger, resentment and frustration continues to grow at an alarming rate, all negative emotions creating an atmosphere of strong, negative energy.

The harshest nature of man can surface when placed in an environment where society has broken down and the citizens ignore the laws of humanity. They justify their actions saying that the laws are not enforced, or cannot be enforced. This state of condition leads to further disintegration of our ability to live in a civilized manner. This impediment has an adverse effect on everyone living there. More people become embittered and antagonistic over the events and pivot toward violence as a symbolizes to resolve the quandary which only induces more hostility. The only way to eliminate this negativity is to withdraw from the cradle of conflict by relocating to a more positive environment, such as found in small towns or more open areas of lesser population.

The preceding material suggests that there are many ways that people have embraced religion, both structured and unstructured, some religions are nature based, others are based on religious books written long ago. We have witnessed the extremely negative side of humanity as radical, Islamic fundamentalists attacked and killed Americans for the pleasures promised them in the Garden of Allah, for doing such deeds. We have also had the privilege of witnessing a more positive side of human nature, with the peaceful worshiping of nature by those are Wiccans and those who follow the Red Road.

We have examined many roads that draw upon the exercise of magic in their rituals and ceremonies. The application of transcendental techniques provides the intensity and the visualization necessary for the magic to become effective within our lives. Magic did not originate from the Middle Ages, but can be found dated back for thousands of year and is a vital part of our continued human existence. We are interconnected to everyone and to all things in this life. We discovered that magic is not restricted to sages, shamans, medicine men, witches or wizards, but is available to anyone who is willing to learn the techniques to activate it within themselves. Magic is as natural as a lovely evening sunset, or as inspiring as a view from a mountain top.

The following chapters will teach you about this magical gift that we all have been endowed with from our creator. You will learn how to take control of your life by applying the principles found in magic. Magic will work if you believe it will work, enhancing life to the fullest. We will share the physics of miracles as we show how quantum mechanics explain why magic will work.

Magic in the Middle Ages

The Pagan Magic Era was a time of great magical happening and a time of great miracles. Magic was an accepted reality and a natural part of the daily lives of the people during the Middle Ages. The early sorcerers, wizards, witches, sages, shamans and magician worked magic because they recognized and utilized the natural flowing energies found in nature. Paganism was accepted and practiced without question or concern. The pagan beliefs were varied depending on their cultural origins.

The contender during this era of magic, were the leaders of the early Christian Church. The Church had transformed from a theological institution to the political, economic and religious enterprise that proclaimed it held the power of God to save or condemn the souls of men and women. The church achieved this position by creating an alignment between the Church and the State, thereby creating an effective dominion that dictated the proper theological structure. Once jurisdictional authority was established, eradication procedures were quickly put into place that would exterminate practitioners of pagan magic by the process of absorption. This practice of absorption enabled those who were recruited by force to join the Church to continue observing their pagan holidays and celebrations, but now under the blessed framework of Christianity.

Church law became the law of the land and anyone who disagreed with the Church found themselves on the proverbial chopping block. A special Church Doctrine Enforcement Corp was established known as the Inquisition in 1231 by Pope Gregory IX as a separate tribunal, independent of bishops and prelates. Its administrators, the inquisitors, were to be answerable only to the Pope. In return for these Doctrine

Enforcement services, the executioners kept a percent of the assets they stripped from the condemned which included, land, cattle, money and anything else of value while the Church took title to the balance of the property and assets. The magical era disappeared as any association with witchcraft was punishable by death. The Inquisitors resembled in practice to the feared Nazi Gestapo, the secret police of Hitler. The Inquisitors were the authorized executioners or assassins used by the Church to ensure conformity and obedience to the doctrines of the Church enforceable by torture and death.

The Inquisition drove the magical movement underground in order to survive. The practice of witchcraft became a capital offense with the infliction of bizarre and brutal torment before death ended the beastly ordeal. Those convicted of witchcraft were not dealt within a humane manner, but made to suffer the most barbaric acts the Church executioners could employ. The magical arts became hidden from society, thus the term occult or hidden came to be used to describe the magical arts. The Church went from an institution of religious rituals and doctrine to a political and economic enterprise that tyrannized the lives of men, women and children, determining what was acceptable, both morally and theologically. This was the beginning of the Dark Ages and the beginning of the confiscation of assets by the Church in the name of God.

Magic was real and the Church had to admit that magic worked, but in doing so, they quickly credited the power of magic to Satan. The magic was considered the shadow form of miracles. Therefore anything associated with magic was deemed to be of a Satanic nature and henceforth evil. This duality of good and evil reached it zenith during the Middle Ages as the Church condemned to death those that were perceived as servants of Satan and confiscated the assets of the condemned. These were truly the dark days of Christianity.

In our own country, the Salem Witch Trials of 1692 ended with the hanging of nineteen people accused of being witches simply because they were different. History also records that the pious religious leaders of Salem, Massachusetts also hung two dogs that were thought to be witch familiars. Unlike the Christians, pagan practitioners never murdered innocent people because they did not accept the pagan earth-based religion. Paganism taught love, healing and harmony while the Christian Church undertook a more fatalistic approach to those who were differed with their tenets.

Through the centuries, people began to believe that God was removed from and condescending of the physical world, they lost their reverence for nature. The perception of time changed so that it no longer seemed related to the seasonal cycles, but to a linear system, consistent with the teachings of the Church. The Church doctrines promoted fear, guilt and obedience. The fear of God that salvation would be lost if they dabbled in magic, guilt because they were sinners and obedience to the church, else they would be cast from the presence of God.

Magic and Cycles

We know that the greater part of the human body is made up of water or liquids. If a 165-pound man was reduced to its basic elements, we would have 65 pounds of various elements and 100 pounds of liquids. Therefore, like the water of Earth, we are affected by the Moon and her phases. Just as the ocean tides are controlled by the lunar cycles, so too is the human body. The type of energy from the phases of the Moon will be echoed in our bodies. There is a hard way and an easy way of accomplishing an objective. The easy way is to time the working with the *Force* when the lunar cycles will enhance the energy levels compared to working with the *Force* during a time of lower energy levels. Remember that at a high tide, the ocean is at its highest level on shore and at a low tide, the ocean has receded far from shore.

We have correlated the importance of understanding lunar cycles for conducting ghost investigations. In our book, *Haunted Reality*, published in 1996 and in our *Home Study Course for Certified Ghost Hunter*, we discuss that one of the peak periods for ghost activity is 3:00 A.M. and that a few days on each side of the new and full moons represent the peak times of the month. Since that book, we have also discovered that solar flares and geomagnetic storms are ideal times for conducting ghost investigations. We are influenced by the geomagnetic fields of the earth in one way or another.

The charged particles bombarding the earth provide the necessary energy to enable the spirits of the dead to manifest in the physical realm. Through our research, we have discovered and released the first models that provided tangible analysis establishing a direct relationship between solar storms and intensified paranormal activities. Since our announcement and through our web site and online newsletter, more than a million visitors have been taught about solar storms in relationship to conducting field investigations. The spirits of the dead are utilizing this excess energy to enable them to access and function within our dimension. Why is it more difficult to think that we can also harness this energy and use it for our benefit?

We are sensitive to solar flares and unsettled geomagnetic conditions resulting from solar flares and magnetic storms as we experience headaches. If the geomagnetic fields of the earth can be detected and influenced by the human body, how much more can be accomplished if we direct and amplify the natural energies about us? The timing is everything when it comes to working with the *Force*.

It is traditional in pagan ceremonies for decrease or removal of problems take place from after the Full Moon until the New Moon, with the day or night of the New Moon being strongest. This would be called waning or declining. Pagan ceremonies for increase, growth and gain take place from after the New Moon until the Full Moon, with the day or night of the Full Moon being the most powerful. This would be called waxing or increasing.

There are those in pagan traditions that will extend the timing of events to the planetary alignment as related to astrology. Each day, each hour is assigned a ruler or in other words, a relationship exists between the hour and planet as it relates to sunrise and sunset. For the purposes of teaching our magic, we will not delve into this aspect of planetary timing. We have found it is not necessary to extend timing factors to planetary configurations.

In Wicca, most practitioners believe it could take up to two weeks for their spells to be effective. This is the time between the New moon and the Full moon. The Language of Prayer does not take two weeks to become effective, but is immediate. In one case a woman had a tumor. She had three mystics work on her by their visualizing an outcome that did not have the tumor. The tumor was shown on a television screen as an ultrasound scan was continuously revealing the shape and size of the tumor. As people watched, the tumor got smaller and smaller and simply vanished from view on the screen. The total elapsed time were two minutes and forty seconds!

Quantum mechanics do not state that replacing one state of outcome with another outcome takes time to be assimilated into our dimension. Laboratory experiments show that this process happens immediately. In this regard, our techniques do not suggest a time lag between the ritual and its fulfilment. We do not believe that the timing is slow, but that the focus and visualization can cause the event to take place immediately. However, if the visualization and focus include a delayed response to correspond with the lunar cycles, than that will be the result. We are the architects of our lives and what we believe will happen. We are only limited by our minds and our beliefs.

The analogy of a radio set with a large dial that can tune in any dimensional frequency is not dependent on a time delay to detect the new dimensional frequency station. When the frequency is set, access is granted immediately. We could say that the dimensional frequencies are like a dimensional Internet connection. When you click on the link, the Internet connects to that link immediately and the web site comes to life on your monitor. These dimensional links are the key to accessing the dimensional sites. The links are created when we focus, concentrate and visualize the site we want to access. This is the science of magic and miracles that we know as the Language of Prayer.

Acceptance of Magic

As society moved away from the nature-based religions and into a non-nature religion that proclaimed nature was an enemy to man, the sensitivities to these native power sources were forgotten and later lost to mankind. Today we bombard our skies with millions of electromagnetic signals generated from radio and television transmitters, massive high-power tension lines and microwave relay stations for telecommunications.

If we add millions of smaller powered transmitters, such as the sixty cycle hums from car alternators, regular power lines that run to every home in this country and all of the electrical devices we have in our home and the RF noises from cellar telephones, we can immediately see that our atmosphere is being jammed with countless signals that are far stronger than those being generated by nature. We live in a state of constant energy bombardment that we have to learn to shield our minds against and tune into the connectedness that is all about us.

Our busy life style, stressful work situations and long hours in traffic have numbed us to the natural energies all about us. Many people have to take time out of their busy schedule to find a place of peace so they can recharge their batteries. Some need a physical recharge while others need a spiritual recharge. However, once the batteries are recharged, most people do not work at becoming receivers for the energies about them. They go back to work in a stressful field, until the next time they have to escape to recharge themselves. We all know that batteries can only be recharged so many times before they wear out!

We have lost touch with nature and its natural flowing energies. Recall how energizing it was the last time you stood on the beach and watched the ocean waves, or stood by waterfall, or a rushing river.

These sources release negative ions that provide us with positive energy making us feel better. Even a shower with the water spraying over us releases negative ions that seem to help revitalize us. We are coming into contact with the *Force* during these times, not even understanding what was happening.

The *Force* is not reserved for wizards, witches, sages, shamans, sorcerers, priests, medicine men or those who enter an altered state of consciousness to experience the energy. It is available to everyone who will follow the techniques and believe that it will work. Many pagan rituals include magical spells and chants that allow an individual to access this energy stream. For some people, there exists a need for a structured event for the left brain to assimilate as the right brain acts upon the symbolic instructions. If the left brain is distracted then the right brain is free to act upon the symbolic instructions. The idea of immediate results may be unrealistic for some individuals to accept, so the slower ritualistic procedures provide the pace that is acceptable and credible. Our own individual experiences will provide either barriers or a lack of barriers within us as to how we envision the timing to be. For some, results should take weeks, or half a lunar cycle, but to others, results should be immediate. Our minds create the realities we accept so we can feel comfortable with the timing. It is not a right or wrong belief, but rather, a synchronizing of events that feels right and comfortable to our inner selves.

Today some religions use magic as part of their ceremonies, not calling it magic, but sacred rites or rituals. The Catholic Church has a ceremony called Mass, where members partake of a wafer and wine offered by the priest. The faithful are told that when they eat of the wafer and drink the wine, they are actually partaking of the body and blood of Christ. The priest believes that the wafer and wine are transmuted into the actual body and blood of Christ. Ancient wizards would call this transmutation, a form of Alchemy. We all know that the most popular Alchemy that wizards searched for, was the secret recipe to turn lead into gold. Alchemy later evolved into the science of

Chemistry. The magic of alchemy is alive and well in the Catholic Church as part of their holy rites and rituals.

In Europe, the Catholic Church still employs the Sin Burning ritual whereby members write their sins on a sheet of special paper and burn it with special candles to rid the member of those sins listed on the paper. This is considered a sacred ceremony, but it is still a magic ritual that is employed by witches and Pagan religions today. The concept of writing your problems on a sheet of parchment and then burning it as you chant words that banish the problem was a pre-Christian ritual absorbed into the Christian Church. Always consider the source of a ceremony and generally it will predate the Christian era and will involve magic in some form.

Shamanism is probably the oldest role in pagan religion that is known to have existed. Cave paintings in South France depict men in animal skins performing a hunting ritual. The cave paintings have been dated to BC 35,000 and show the imitations and participation with the animals and the natural world. While we do not know what their rituals consisted of, the important aspect is not the rituals themselves, but the emotional energy that was focused into them.

Whether our Paleolithic ancestors came to North American across the Great Land Bridge or sailed from Asia to land on the Western coast of North America, they brought their ceremonies and cultural beliefs with them. In time, the tribes spread across the continent and the ceremonies and beliefs changed according to the local environment. Some tribes became dependent on the land and raised crops. Their shamans would seek spirits of the elements for good harvests. The shaman of hunting tribes would seek the spirits of the animals they were seeking. The shaman would enter an altered consciousness generally considered to be the lower world where they could converse with the spirits and seek guidance for their people from friendly spirits. Shamans would perform magic for their tribal members, where often healing included herbal remedies, which were considered holy rituals by those who did not understand the process.

Paleolithic big game hunters practiced their form of paganism from BC 13,000 according to findings in one Middle Tennessee archaeological site. The local environment influenced the evolution of the ceremonies and rituals performed. Some ceremonies were based on mythologies that bypassed regional areas. For example, the Earth Diver myth that described the creation of land and its people, can be found in Asia and in the Midwest and Southeast of the United States, but not in the Pacific Northwest or the Southwest. Other ceremonies were based on regional animals, such as in the Pacific Northwest where Indians held the Salmon sacred and the Plains Indians held the Buffalo sacred because these were the creatures that provided life to the tribes.

The Native Americans or Native people today practice a belief system that has been called, *Medicine Way, Natural Way and the Red Road*, a spiritual practice that unites body, mind, spirit and nature within their Circle of Life. Just as the visionary and medicine man *Black Elk*, shared his vision of the Circle of Life that he described as the Sacred Hoops or circles within circles. The interconnectedness of all things, both above and below.

In recent years, especially since Wicca was declared to be a legal religion, the pagan, earth-based religions have been on the upswing. We find more books published today that are written about magic and witchcraft than ever before. It is now time for a book on the Language of Prayer that connects all the pagan ceremonies like dots on a page resulting in the total appearing greater than the sum of its parts. Each has a portion to contribute, all contributing toward a whole.

We are constantly asked how ghosts can be reconciliated with Christianity, especially those Christian sects that teach ghosts are fallen spirits from the grace of God? As we pointed out previously, religion deals with the outward ordinates of worship, rituals, doctrines and congregational practices, yet does not deal with the spiritual side of life. Ghosts are denizens of the spiritual realm or we could suggest, another space-time dimension, and therefore they will be an enigma to Christianity. The same question will be asked about magic. How can it be reconciliated with Christianity? Again, the response would be the same. Magic is an enigma, a puzzle to Christianity, because the very foundation of religion is built upon destroying the nature-man link that our ancestors enjoyed. Perhaps the question should be how can magic be reconciliated with God and not to a man-made belief system?

Magic is not in conflict with God and never has been. Magic is simply the application of natural laws that can be understood by applying quantum mechanics. Quantum mechanics may seem like magic to many who study its precepts and tenets. Mathematical equations testify to the validity of quantum mechanics, but it has only been recently that laboratory experiments have confirmed the mathematical equations that proposed quantum mechanics. Many who study this branch of science will readily admit that it sounds like magic compared to classical physics.

The working of magic requires that the practitioner take control of his or her life. This is a difficult transition for some who are caught up in the fast lane of life. Busy schedules, demanding pressures of employment and family life leaves little time for relaxation and meditation. Many people are abandoning the fast lane of city life and seeking the slower paced lifestyles in rural America. While not everyone can leave their employment in the cities and move to rural towns, the concepts presented in this book do enable them to take charge of their lives and realize that they can become more grounded and balanced by application of the techniques presented later in this book.

One of the positive features of applying this magic is that the individual will experience the energy flow from themselves and from nature. They need to become attuned to their inner selves, their soul and the care of their soul. The techniques discussed are very important and provide the training to establish control over your own powers. A sail boat without a rudder is at the mercy of the wind, blowing in the direction of the wind. However, if we add a rudder to the sailboat, we can navigate by the principle of tacking, or using the rudder and the wind to zig zag to the desired destination. Sometimes zig zagging to the destination is faster than trying to sail in a straight course. Magic is much like a sailboat, sometimes it employs rituals and chants to zig zag to reach the objective.

When we say spells and chants, most people think of something evil or a wicked old witch stirring a boiling cauldron. Hollywood has stereotyped and tainted the understanding of spells and chants. In Church, we may sing songs of praise to an invisible God, and no one thinks anything of it. However, chant similar words and call it a spell and it is magically transformed into something dubious. We must break out of this kind of mind set and allow our minds to be clear and free of negative anchors imposed on us by those who would keep us from knowing the secrets of our inner power. We talk about labels applied to procedures and immediately someone will react because of a previous mind set established by fear or by lack of understanding.

Consider that the American Indians were looked upon as heathens by the white men who came west to settle the land. This invading army of settlers deemed the Native Americans as savages because their religion was earth based and not a Christian-based religion. Hence, they were exterminated or if treaties were established, those treaties were broken time and again and Indian people regarded the white men as liars. Indian schools were established, but were nothing more than places for cruel and inhumane treatment of Indian boys and girls where their culture and traditional ways of life were taken away. Their native beliefs were deemed wrong and unchristian so the white man's version of God was imprinted into them. Today we finally have a better, clearer comprehension that the Indians were not all savages, but were more civilized than the white man. Prejudices died hard, but prejudices are negative mind sets, not based on facts, but upon fears.

Similarly, magic must be approached with an open mind, our prejudices buried and our minds as fertile ground ready for planting. We must leave behind our fears of labels and the teachings of misinformed groups as we allow ourselves to understand the wonderful power of the *Force*. This magic will change our lives, but we have to believe we have the power to do so. This is not a realm for skeptics or the negative thinkers. Magic is real if you will but believe it is real.

As in Star Wars, Luke Skywalker has the power of the Force, but he lacks confidence and knowledge of how to use it. He had to make the conscious decision that he wanted to be trained in the ways of a Jedi Warrior. In comes Yoda who is a Jedi Master. Yoda is to train Luke Skywalker in the ways of the Force. Each of us is a Luke Skywalker, we have the power of the Force, but we lack the knowledge of how to develop and implement it. The *Force* is with us all, we simply have to reach out and learn how to use it.

We need to understand that all things are made of energy. Our thoughts and feelings are nothing more than energy patterns. The Language of Prayer specifically discusses the importance of thoughts and feelings as key ingredients for achieving successful outcomes. Our choices in life determine the direction of the nature of our thoughts, feelings and actions.

Consider the following example. Feelings of joy and despair are nothing more than energy of a certain magnitude. When choices are made, the energies making up the feelings of joy or despair take on direction. These diametric feelings are one and the same, nothing more than energy that has been assigned a direction through choice. Each of us has energy within us that remains neutral until we assign feelings or energy to it. Depending on the feelings, joy or despair, the direction will be opposite for each, but the magnitude will be the same. The energy is not good or bad, but represents potential that can be released in any direction we choose.

As we approach problems in life, we may need to examine the function rather than the effect of the choice we make. An example is a commonly posed question that reflects one's outlook on life: "Is the glass half-empty or half-full?" Are we asking the right question? Should we ask: "Is the glass the right size?" The glass could be too large or too small. If we look at decisions as a set of opposites on a linear continuum, it may lead a person away from understanding the continuum itself.

We live in a world of cycles, circles within circles representing an interconnectedness to all things. The circle should be the continuum we view our problems within. Our lives do not exist within a linear continuum with past followed by present followed by future, with all behind us vanishing away forever. The decisions we make today will affect the generations to come after us. Our decisions must consider the circle of life, and the repeating of life cycles from one generation to the next. How will our choices today affect our children and grandchildren of tomorrow? We are all connected, from one generation to the next. It is when we forget that connectedness that we lose our balance and harmony with nature and with ourselves. We have forgotten this interconnectedness and now we are suffering the consequences of poorly planned government programs relating to how we are treating our planet in relationship to clean air and water. What are we doing for the next generation?

Magic Dimensions will help to restore that harmony and balance we have lost. Life is filled with problems, challenges and difficulties for that is the nature of life. Our task is to learn how to smooth out the ripples caused by the problems, challenges and difficulties. In nature when a stone is tossed into a pond, the resulting ripples will radiate outward until those ripples come into contact with other solid objects and bounce back toward the source. The reflecting ripples will neutralize the forward-moving ripples returning the pond back to balance and harmony. Our lives can return to harmony and balance. We have the power within us to make these changes.

The magic can effect changes in nature, in ourselves and in others. The outcome of that magic can be for good or for bad, the energy is the same, it is just how we apply it that determines the direction. The Native people and Wiccans have similar creeds, do what you want, but harm none. *Magic Dimensions* is about understanding yourself, your inner voice and how you are connected to everyone else in this Circle of Life. Sharon had a dream during the writing of this book. She described her dream as marbles rolling around inside a dish. The dish is the Circle of Life and the marbles represent each of us because we are all interconnected We are like marbles rolling around together in a big dish.

The Source of Magic

Magic is not a slight of hand illusion or of consorting with a mythical devil, but magic is the application of natural laws, to create the magic. For many years, scientists consider the world flat and would not accept any other explanation. Science is still in its infancy when it comes to understanding the relationship between man and nature. Science is exploring the tip of an iceberg when it comes to understanding about quantum mechanics and parallel dimensions. Yet the understanding of quantum mechanics is essential in understanding the Language of Prayer and understanding the Language of Prayer is essential in understand the *Force* and magic itself.

We all need magic in our lives. Unfortunately we have lived so long without magic that any miracle is beyond our comprehension, so we ascribe it to God. This has become the proverbial catch all for all unexplained phenomena in our Western culture. Miracles are simply the results of applying magical techniques that generate the outcome we were seeking for. If we strike a wooden match on a hard surface, the match will ignite. The fire was not a miracle from God, but not understand the science behind it, it remained miraculous nonetheless. Some thought the resulting flame, the work the devil. The match was called a Lucifer by the cowboys of the West prior to the Civil War. Today we understand that the match head is composed of chemical compounds that when fiction is applied will ignite. This process is a natural chemical reaction, yet in the past, the resulting flame was considered a miracle from God or from Satan depending on who had the flame.

Since starting this book, we have been contacted by people who are desperate for help. The solution to their problems lies within these pages. Some may be facing serious medical procedures or severe medical disorders that are both painful and debilitating. The medical profession is not always able to resolve the problem and it seems as if prayer is the only recourse. But, traditional prayers sometimes fail to achieve the miraculous results needed. Others may find themselves on a treadmill going nowhere. The magic contained in this book will enable a transformation to take place that will realign your life to one of your choosing. Do not doubt what you will read and learn, for it is the way that magic will come into your life. We have found these principles and techniques to be very effective at the working of magic. You are invited to learn and apply the magic herein.

Magic Dimensions is not about a theological doctrine or a religious ritual, but is the spiritual, dimensional approach to evoke a different future outcome of our choosing. *Magic Dimensions* does not deny or validate God any more than the Law of Gravity validates or denies God, but it does represent the application of natural laws found within quantum mechanics. What do we mean when we say natural laws? We are suggesting that the understanding we have of the Language of Prayer can be explained by the strange and weird behavior of subatomic particles within quantum mechanics. Quantum mechanics have also been called quantum weirdness because it goes beyond what was thought possible in Classical Physics when we approach the subatomic realm.

The laws of Classical Physics do not apply in the subatomic realm. A complete new set of understandings was required. In time, a new set of theories was mathematically developed that explained the behavior of the subatomic domain. As our understanding evolved, so did our knowledge of other dimensions. Today we have observed and mathematically proven that natural laws are being observed in quantum mechanics. The weirdness is not a supernatural phenomenon, meaning that is lies outside of natural laws, but resides within the natural laws. The Language of Prayer falls within the natural laws defined by quantum mechanics and is therefore not supernatural or paranormal. If it is not supernatural or paranormal then it cannot be attributed to God, but must be accepted as a natural effect of a natural law.

The construct of prayer that is described in the Christian Bibles, including all past and present translations are a corrupted interpretation of the original language and techniques practiced by the Essence community nestled along the Red Sea some five hundred years before the advent of the Christian era. Any remaining vestiges of that ancient language were lost in AD 325 as the Council of Nicaea removed all references to the True Language of Prayer and inserted the abridged version. While it is not known the psychology behind this deliberate removal of the techniques, we could speculate that the pious council members felt threatened and therefore they endeavored to destroy the secrets of performing this magic for fear that it would undermine or destroy their political and economic power base.

We have undertaken to expose the foundation that the Christian Church is based upon. This foundation is not absolute and did not originate from God, but from other nature-based religions. The Holy Bible is not absolute as many would teach, but represents a collection of books that were acceptable in AD 325 to the King. Hundreds of other books were banished or destroyed during this reconstruction period of Christianity, especially those texts relating to Gnostic Christians who were a threat to the orthodox Christians. Christianity evolved, not as an inspired religion, but as a powerful political and economic organization that allowed the Church to assume a position equal with the King. Thus, we have over 2,200 Christian sects today contenting with each other for the control of the flock.

In our times, many men have discovered that this magical energy is interconnected to everything around us. This interconnectedness of all things is not new, we have shown that even our indigenous people believed and acted according to this concept as did those who practiced paganistic rituals half a millennium before Christianity. We have in our generation the inventions of Henry Moray and Nikola Tesla who each demonstrated a working device that generated electricity directly from the surrounding air. Imagine, free energy. Now guess who would not want free energy to be made available to the public? History reveals that both men were not allowed to bring their discoveries to the attention of the public. When Tesla died, his apartment was closed by order of National Security and all of his papers, both personal and working and his models, were confiscated by the government, perhaps stored in that great secret warehouse, away from public access. But the government has demonstrated, by their own development, that Teslas's ideas worked and work well for the agenda they hold sacred. The HAARP Project is one good, working example of Tesla's discoveries.

We face the same concerns today with fossil fuel prices skyrocketing, yet the crude oil price has remained stable. The skyrocketing prices are being manipulated by the oil companies, the middle men and the gas distributors. The consumer is forced to pay the price set by the gas distributors. Ask yourself this question. If the price of crude oil stays the same, why is the market value of the gas changing so drastically? We were originally told it was due to crude oil prices, but now that explanation appears to be just window dressing. Crude oil prices are now the same as they were in the mid 1980's when the price of gasoline was under a dollar a gallon. Why?

Cold Fusion came along and the inventors were force to leave American soil and go to France to continue their work. The major oil companies would not like to see Cold Fusion become available to the general public because it would eliminate the need for fossil fuels. Eliminate the need for fossil fuel and too many powerful people and companies would be threatened. Thus, they will do whatever it takes at whatever cost to survive. Money and power are still the driving forces today in big business. The same scenario fits in with the religious sector and when looking at the overall pattern throughout history, it is power, financial gain and control that stand out clearly.

Now lets address the issues surrounding magic itself. Magic works because of the *Force*. The *Force* has many names, such as Psychokinesis (PK), Scalar Waves, Hyper-dimensional Physics, the Energy of Life,

Sea of Energy, Chi, Prana, Zero Point Energy, Orgone, Biofield, and a dozen other names given to this power by scientists and researchers. This *Force* or energy is a resonance or alignment between the consciousness and the physical reality. The physical reality encompasses all domains or dimensions.

Robert G. Jahn, a professor of aerospace science and dean emeritus of the School of Engineering and Applied Science at Princeton University, suggests that reality is itself the result of the bridge between the wavelike features of consciousness and the wave pattern of matter. Clinical psychologist Brenda Dunne, an associate of Jahn, suggests that this transmission of energy involves an exchange of information between the consciousness and physical realities, an exchange that is more of a resonance between the two.

University of London physicist David Bohm, a protege of Einstein's and one of the worlds most respected Quantum Physicists, found a strange state of interconnectedness that seemed to exist between apparently unrelated subatomic happenings. While at the Berkeley Radiation Laboratory, Bohm discovered that once electrons were in a plasma, they were part of a larger and interconnected whole. The individual movement of these electrons appeared random, yet vast numbers of electrons were able to exhibit effects that were arrayed in an organized manner. Later Bohm commented on his impression that the electron sea was "alive." Bohm believes matter does not exist independent from the sea of energy, but matter is like a ripple on this interstellar sea of energy.

The power of this dynamic sea of energy can be focused and projected either directly with the mind, or when applied in ritualistic or ceremonial settings that involve the casting of spells, chants and enchantments as a prelude to the focusing and projecting of this energy. Resonance can be achieved by both techniques, depending upon which mode feels more comfortable for the practitioner. We have used both techniques and found of them to work successfully. Magic comes in many constructs because the energy can be applied in different ways. The rituals and chants are very significant to those belief systems that incorporate them. Alignment with ritualistic ceremonies will access the same energy flow as those who use the Language of Prayer. This is the Yin and the Yang, the two sides of the coin. One is not better than the other, both are equal but follow different sets of protocols.

The *Force* is every where and in every time. It is found in nature and in our own bioplasmic fields. The *Force* is simply a term to identify the collective natural energy that is the magical component in magical rituals. Whether this energy can be correlated with a Unified Energy Theory is left to the men of science who invest their life times attempting to prove mathematically these kinds of relationships. Physicists, such as Fred Hoyle, Fred Alan Wolf, Stephen Hawking and John Gribbin, have and are exploring time, parallel universes, black holes, superstrings, wormholes and the Unification of Physics. In time we may have the mathematics as to why the Language of Prayers works, but for now, we do not have to concern ourselves with these scientific areas. It is simply enough to know that many leading physicists are continuously proving various aspects of this Language of Prayer.

Quantum mechanics is a new term, but in the past Metaphysics has been explored by such men as Richard Hoagland, Nikola Testa, Moray King, Henry Moray, Thomas Bearden, Harold Aspden and many others. This new physics uses zero-point-energy devices that enable the invisible to become visible. The zero-point-energy is a term reflecting the medium that previously had been referred to as, ether by scientists of the eighteenth and nineteenth centuries. This Zero-point-energy is considered an energetic, random fluctuation of electric flux imbedded with the fabric of space. Magical ceremonies simply orient the direction and magnitude of this electric flux.

The theory of ether describes space as a sea of fluctuating energy. Physicist use zero-point-energy to describe this sea of energy because at zero-point Kelvin these fluctuations remain active. We no longer call this sea of energy ether, but instead, refer to this sea of energy as zero-point energy. This electric flux is what we are calling the *Force*. Regardless of the name we apply to this sea of energy that is all around us, we can tap into that energy source by the techniques we will describe in this book. We are all interconnected to this *Force* and this *Force* is interconnected to all dimensions, our own and all parallel dimensions because the *Force* is the energy that connects all things. As the great Oglala Sioux visionary and medicine man Black Elk said in his vision, "circles within circles."

One of the first lessons we teach in this book is as follows: Magic works if you believe it will. We are skeptical by nature, but if we learn to silence that skepticism so that our minds become open to the knowledge and endless possibilities, we can experience the benefits of working with magic. As we stated earlier, magic can be achieved in one of two ways. The first is to apply and live the Language of Prayer. This may be difficult for some since the Language of Prayer is a direct application of quantum mechanics and may require a leap of faith that some cannot muster. The second way that magic can be achieved is much older and relies upon deceiving the left analytical brain by the use of rituals, chants and icons so the right creative brain can implement the symbolic instructions directly to the subconscious mind. We will discuss more of the second method in detail later in the book.

Consider Aleister Crowley's definition of magic, paraphrased as the act of causing change to conform to one's purpose. Magic is the ability to intentionally effect changes at the quantum level, to prepare oneself to intentionally observe the desired outcome, in order to manifest measurable effect. The art of spell casting puts the caster into a state of condition that allows the person to alter the probability of an action occurring, choosing some outcome that is less likely to be allowed by the classical physics of our world. When a practitioner of magic focuses his or her will in the casting of a spell, he or she initiates change at a subatomic level. The user of magic effects the probability of an event. The practitioner of magic becomes the observer, selecting an actual outcome from the myriad of probable outcomes. Magic is not really magic, it is merely an application of natural rules we simply do not fully understand. Scientist and author Arthur Clark's Third Law states: "Any sufficiently advanced technology is indistinguishable from magic." Perhaps an inversion of Clark's Third Law would read: "Any sufficient advanced magic is indistinguishable from technology."

The *Force* can be understood by comprehending the *Magic Dimensions*. We can define *Magic Dimensions* as the changing of future events by applying techniques that cause a dimensional shift resulting in a transformation from the old reality to the creation of a new reality that is superimposed into our time stream. This is a displacement of the old reality and the acquisition of a new reality established by our specifications. Stephen Hawking, Lucasian Professor of Mathematics at the University of Cambridge and widely esteemed as the most brilliant Theoretical Physicist since Einstein, wrote in *A Brief History of Time* that "Quantum mechanics do not predict a single definite result...Instead, it predicts a number of different possible outcomes and tells us how likely each of these is."

The transformation process involves the application of the *Force*. We had said earlier that the practice of magic means the projection of natural energies to produce needed effects of our choosing. The key word is 'needed,' not just desired. Desires change like the phases of the moon, but a need is definite and necessary. A need is more profound than simply a want. We all want things, but if we do not need it, it will not come to pass. One must learn certain basic techniques: concentration, focusing, meditation and imaging. It is not merely learning these techniques, but the acceptance and faithful discharge of them that will trigger the transcendental event. Practice the techniques until you have perfected the procedures and protocols. Practice creative visualization at every opportunity, the more proficient you become, the more successful will be your outcomes.

The *Force* can be found in nature, along earth fault lines, near flowing water, and from many other manmade sources, such as roads, power lines and railroad lines. I will give some examples of how this *Force* was utilized in geophysical applications. In the early eighties, I was working in the oil and gas fields as a geophysical consultant. I was using a subsurface radar imaging system that delineated subsurface lithology. The system would transmit a VHF radio frequency signal into the earth and a second receiving system would detect the injected signal and by triangulation, the depth of the injected signal could be ascertained. The injected signal was fed into a spectrum analyzer with frequencies calibrated to different subsurface strata's. One of the interesting phenomena that occurred when this signal was injected into the ground and passed through a fault the signal set up a feedback oscillation loop in the receiver. This method of detecting subsurface depth relied upon the same understanding of this *Force* that may have been used by Tesla for his earth transmitter. The interesting aspect of this system was that the scientific understanding of radio waves suggested that a VHF radio frequency signal could not be injected into the earth more than a few hundred feet. The system I was using was injecting signals to over a depth of two miles into the earth. Some considered this to be magic.

Another example of how the *Force* may be detected is the art of Dowsing. Many people can use dowsing rods to find fault lines and water. While no current explanation exists for why dowsing works successfully, we suspect that the dowsing rods when aligned by the human mind in a concentrated, focused objective will respond to this natural energy we call the *Force*. When the dowser walk over faults or cross underground waterways, the rods will cross because the rods react to the electromagnetic energy flowing along the fault lines and along the water channels. Water witchers have used a forked hazel wood branch to locate subsurface deposits of water for centuries. Some water well drillers refuse to drill unless the site has been witched by someone knowledgeable in the art of witching. They have learned from sad experience that their success ratio is higher when the site is found by a water witch who has dowsed the site. My grandfather would dowse for water very successfully. I can remember him cutting a forked branch and walking around the hill looking for water. I remember my dad trying it and how amazed he was that the forked branch seemed to have a life of its own as it pointed downward. Its force was so strong that my dad could not move the point of the branch away from the site. This was a simple application of using the *Force* to find water. It is still a common practice in many areas today, though rarely publicized.

While evaluating an oil and gas lease in Nevada with the above described subsurface radar system, I detected the sixty cycle hum emitting from a fault line. This hum was not being generated by our equipment, nor were there power lines in this remote section of Nevada. I knew this was not a natural occurring phenomena so I decided to track down the origins of this mysterious hum. I traced the fault with my equipment until I discovered a large drilling rig sitting directly on the fault line. The hum was coming from the equipment in operation at that drilling site. The drilling rig was over a mile from the lease I was exploring at the time. The sixty cycle hum was being projected along the fault line through some kind of medium whose matrix was not understood at the time.

Later I developed a passive extremely low frequency spectral analysis imaging system that did not necessitate transmitting a radio signal into the earth. This new ELF system allowed this energy we call the *Force* also known as telluric earth energy to be analyzed by a spectral frequency software program designed to interpret the shift in frequency within this energy flow. This new and passive system would detect subsurface lithology, especially faults and fractures because it worked with the earths geomagnetic fields or telluric fields and the existing electrical energy being generated by manmade power sources. When I operated this system near power lines, I obtained strong readings from fractures and faults. It seems that these faults and fractures conveyed the electrical energy from the power lines and transmitted it along the faults. The faults were very noisy with this electromagnetic energy. The sixty cycle signal from high power lines falls within the Extremely Low Frequency range and has a cycle equal to twenty-five thousand miles or roughly the diameter of the earth. The length of this single sine wave at 60 cycles was the diameter of the earth, in other words, the wave passed through the earth without being blocked.

If I stood over a fault line near a power line, the signal strength of the energy coming from the fault would be significantly stronger than when I moved away from the fault. I have seen patents for oil detection systems based on the use of high-power lines that provided the energy that penetrated into the earth, yet if one were to ask a petroleum geologist about this concept, generally they would discount the concept. The reason is that this concept of telluric energy was never taught in their academic courses. Very few geologists study other science disciplines to find applications that would benefit them in their field of expertise. They rely upon their own vertical industry for knowledge. Major breakthroughs in other scientific disciplines go unnoticed in vertical industries. Scientists are often like skeptics when something new or unique enters the arena. Each will maintain a mind set that is closed to new and revolutionary concepts, especially if not reproducible within the confines of laboratory conditions.

A simple experiment that will access this *Force* or telluric earth energy and confirm the presence of underground faults is as follows: Obtain a gasoline generator and attach a heavy duty electrical cord to the positive and negative sides of the output. At the opposite end of the electrical cord, strip the plastic coating back to reveal the wires inside, separating the colored wires. Drive two four-foot lengths of metal rod three feet into the ground, separating the two rods by at least six feet. Attach one color of wire to one rod and the other to the second rod. A load must be installed in series to prevent short circuiting of the AC current, such as a light socket with a light bulb inserted into the socket. Take any portable AM radio and tune to a dead spot on the dial. Start the generator and start walking around the area with the portable AM radio as you look for a fault or fracture. When you cross such a fracture or fault, the 60 cycle hum can be heard on the radio. The hum or static will increase as you approach the fault and decease as you depart from the fault. This is the same principle as to why the radio will pick up lightening discharges prior to the arrival of a storm. The lightening discharged is at ELF and is transmitted through the earth and detected by the radio in the form of static discharges.

The *Force* seems to be some kind of electrical waveform transmitted at an extremely-low frequency. The interesting aspect to this is that this electrical waveform is also in the extremely low frequencies and therefore will have a wavelength is greater than the diameter of the earth. This means that the signal will pass through the earth without being blocked. The U.S. Navy uses this same principle for communication with their submarines at sea while submerged. They have long wires buried in the ground that run for miles. Nikola Tesla invented a method of communicating through the earth that would be secure from listening ears.

All living entities have electrical fields. We know that Coronal Mass Ejections generate solar storms and solar flares that will bombard the earth with strong magnetic fields. These storms and flares will affect some people with headaches and some people report feeling like they are completely zapped of any energy. These solar storms and flares produce intense charged particles that bombard the Earth's geomagnetic fields. During these times, ghosts are most active. With sensitive meters, one can measure the electrical fields emitting from the human body. Each organ has a vibration rate, at which it resonates when in good health. When that vibration rate changes, the body experiences problems and our health suffers.

When you, acting as a little electrical field or magnet, spin in the Earth's giant geomagnetic field, just like a dynamo you produce a high amount of the *Force* tuned to the speed of the spin. You turn yourself into a minute electromagnetic dynamo and in effect, you can make yourself into a powerfully pulsing magnet. When that magnet moves in the Earth's geomagnetic field, your powers are amplified. The fastest and easiest way to generate additional power, therefore, is to pivot yourself around in a fast spin. This is the principle behind turbines that generate power at dams and other co-generation plants.

The power for magic comes from nature and the elements found in nature. Any living thing has energy that can be drawn upon. The earth has its telluric fields that can also supply energy for the power to work magic. Again magic is the simple application of natural laws. We also have the power within us that we can tap into for a power source. The secret lies in the matrix that is formed when we combine the natural energies, the ceremonies to ensnare the left brain, the symbols to program the right brain and the focus, concentration, meditation and imaging to create a dimensional discontinuity of our choosing. This matrix is the recipe for a successful outcome, but if we leave out an ingredient, then the final product will not be the same.

Understanding the Human Mind

Magic works if you think it works. Therein lies the secret to making magic work for you. You have to believe in it! It is for this reason that skeptics or unbelievers are unable to work any magic because they believe it is impossible and therefore they fail. But failure only comes to those who quit. Magic does work and it will work for you, not slight of hand tricks, but good old fashion magic. To work magic effectively, you must believe you can cause things to happen, that you have the power within you to change your life. You must believe that it is within your power to take a desire, an emotional feeling without physical substance, and manifest it in the physical realm. You are not sheep led by another toward the cliff. You have the right to ask questions, to debate the accuracy of what you are told, and decide for yourself as to the truthfulness and validity of what you hear.

You must become as a small child with an open mind that is ready to be filled with knowledge. The magic you will discover will change your life forever. You will discover for yourself that you have the ability and the talents for great things. All we are doing are showing the protocols that need to be followed to access the Magic. What you do with this magic is your business, we are not your judges nor your confessors. The magic has been working for us and it will work for each person who applies the techniques that we will be sharing with you. You still have the responsibility for your own ethical conduct when it comes to the employment of that magic. The world still needs honest men and women, those who stand for truth and justice. Too many men are caught up with power and money as their objectives in life. This shadow existence does not do well for demonstrating harmony and beauty.

Lets examine the scientific side of why magic will work for you. Our brain is composed of two hemispheres. The left side is the logical and analytical brain that requires instructions to make sense. We can call this side the skeptic or nonbelieiver and the right side of the hemisphere as the creative side, or the believer. The task then becomes how to route instructions about changes that we want to implement that is not rejected by the left brain.

The explanations used in pagan ceremonies provide some insights. The act of magical gesturing, reciting spells and all other physical parts of magic deceive our analytical left brain. It becomes so involved in taking an active, physical, logical part in the ritual, that it forgets to monitor and control the creative activity of the right brain. The right brain and the subconscious mind perform best when presented with symbols. All spells, tokens, motifs, tools, chants, etc. become symbols which the right brain readily accepts and uses to create the desired effect.

The more emotionally involved you are in spell work, the more creative activity happens in the right brain. The more creative activity there is, the stronger the message to the subconscious mind that we definitely desire a specific change to happen. Controlled emotional input in ritual proves to the subconscious mind that you are sincere in your desires and what you are attempting to accomplish.

When working with the *Force*, repetition plays a great part in this implementation. The ancients were wise in their insistence on the magical power numbers of 3, 5, 7 and 9. Doing spell work for 3, 5, 7 or 9 days, consecutively, reinforces the creative activity in the right brain and underlines your message, "I want this to happen!" When we start out working magic, our confidence is still being strengthen by successful outcomes. By repetition, we continue to build our confidence in the magic. Some magic that employs the *Force* may require longer periods for the manifestation to happen because the changes are taking place naturally over time.

To work magic effectively, you must believe you can cause things to happen, that you have the power within you to change your life. You must believe that it is within your power to take a desire, an emotional feeling without physical substance, and manifest it in the physical realm.

The content of the spell is only important so far as it entrains the left brain and enables the right brain to accept and pass through to the subconscious which sends to the super consciousness which acts upon the instructions immediately. Spells are nothing more than an allure to keep the left brain busy while the symbolism and words feed information to the right brain. When we think of spells, we may think of chants, enchantments, incantations, curses and potion brewing in a cauldron, but these are only words that create a harmonic resonance that will trigger the subconscious mind to facilitate the desired outcome. Spells are instructions that help us focus in our Language of Prayer.

We will be using the term *ritual* to mean the Modus Operandi or mode of operation for a ceremony. It is important that the student does not get stuck at this stage of learning. We do not want the terms spells, chants, enchantments, rituals, symbols or any other term that also applies to pagan ceremonies to become a stumbling block because of any negative mind sets to these terms. Sometimes it is easier to use the ancient traditional names than to invent new ones that are politically correct. Once the student understands the principles involved and can perform basic magic spells, then the student should practice on their own combination.

In many witchcraft and pagan ceremonies, elaborate rituals with burning candles, salt, daggers, cauldrons, alters, robes, bells and symbols of masculine and feminine energies or as they say, the Lord and the Lady must be present. In modern Shamanism, ceremonies involving sweat lodges, vision quests or initiation into the Medicine Man

Lodge, may overpower the deeper and more important aspect of the ceremony. Just as in Christianity, some sects are fundamental and by that definition, they are considered to be more radial and pugnacious than their counterparts in main stream Christianity. The most important element of these ceremonies is not the ritualistic patterns followed, but the ability to distract the left logical, analytical brain so the symbolism can be conveyed to the right creative brain who in turn acts on the commands, effecting changes immediately.

The Language of Prayer

We live in an age that emphasizes technological advances and future advancements and possibilities beneficial to our health, well_being and comfort. We await breakthroughs that cure debilitating, even fatal diseases and we are told that the cures are just over the horizon with the strides medical science is making. However, the cures are still not available to the average person, nor will they be for some time. We are given hope of future discoveries, but we must rely upon our own experience that these wonderful cures are still decades away.

In this modern age we see the world in terms of physical assets, material possessions, cash flow, bigger is better, more is an advantage. Happiness comes from what we have and money, well, money is the way of things and has become an icon of worship. Importance is placed on the physical things outside of ourselves. We are told that the three carnal motivators are money, power and sex. These are the base motivations that drive the human race if we allow our humanity to take a back stage to our primal instincts.

But there comes a time in our lives, generally as we grow older, that we stop and look around us, wondering what this life is all about. We find our "things" don't hold the meaning that they once did, our comfort and joy doesn't lie in the material possessions around us. In truth, it takes one catastrophic event to take material possessions from us. It is then we realize that those "things" don't give us meaning, that it isn't the "things" that make us who we really are.

The biggest question of all becomes, "Who am I?" We search for ourselves and our purpose, for true and lasting happiness. We desire more profound knowledge of ourselves and the world around us and so begins the journey that can bring change and wisdom. This is a time of transition and opportunity. Transition means changes and human beings hate changes. We like our ruts, our levels of comfort as we avoid changes.

Sometimes we are thrown into transitions by the tragedies that enter into our lives. We lose a child, spouse, parents or we find ourselves losing our security such as a job, home, family, or a marriage where we felt ourselves secure. Whatever is taken from us in such a dramatic way, changes what we have become accustom to being a normal part of our existence.

We soon discover that nothing in this life is permanent and what we have around us may give us a sense of comfort and joy, but can be taken very quickly. What we have around us, is not who we are. Our things do not comprise the beings we are, deep within. It sometimes takes a tragedy or experiencing the harsher side of life to bring us to a place of going inward and connecting with our inner selves, the true nature of whom we are.

We have made great technological strides and yet in the process we have lost much. We have lost touch with ourselves, our true nature, each other and the purpose of sharing this world together. We have forgotten the importance of feelings, of helping one another, of seeing the loving touch of God in the beauty that surrounds us, in nature and in each individual we encounter.

Have you taken the time to stop and smell the roses today? To see each rose petal for the beauty it holds? To find yourself in full awareness of all that surrounds you that gives a true sense of peace and fulfillment deep within you? It is this heightened awareness that fills your soul that can render answers to the questions you ponder.

It is the simplicity in life that brings the soul to fulfillment. It is the hardship that brings added joy and thankfulness to our prosperity. With the hardships come wisdom and that wisdom gives us the insights to true joy, peace and harmony. Life is subject to change at any given moment.

There are three key parts of every human being that make us who we are and create the circumstances of our lives. These three things are; thought, feelings and emotions. They effect us and everything around us, including our destinies. These are the keys not only to our humanity but also to our spirituality. The decisions we make every day, take us in certain directions in our lives. Quantum theory suggests that there exist many outcomes for any given moment in time. We create the conditions that attract future outcomes that have already been established, to the present time, rather than creating our reality.

We may feel that our lives are headed in a certain direction, our daily thoughts and decisions pertain to that direction and goal. Yet that path can change at any time to produce another outcome, one that we have not anticipated. It is where we place our attention, the redirection of our focus that brings a new course of events to us. Throughout our lives, we change. Our likes, our dislikes, our desires, goals, needs, environment, in other words we are variable. As we change, so change existing courses of events that no longer hold a purpose for us. These changes are subtle and so natural that we most likely never recognize when we cross over into a new outcome. If a choice or decision we make is spontaneous or natural, the change allows us new experiences and possibilities we had only dreamed of in the past. Prayer is the language that allows us to express our dreams and desires, bringing them to reality.

Realistically, people are followers. From birth we begin the long process of learning, but that learning is structured on tradition and is limited. As we age, experience becomes a greater teacher. We may find we discard what we have been shown if we find no proof of its validity. We may embark on a new path, embracing the opportunities of a new way, if we find evidence that it is a better path for us.

When we allow ourselves to accept new possibilities, it is that moment of choice when the magic begins. If you make a decision to learn more about ghosts and the human spirit that lives on after the physical body has ceased living, in a world that basically is unaccepting of this subject, you will discover a new direction toward a new outcome.

The Language of Prayer is an incredibly strong mechanism for achieving transcendental progressions. While ordinary prayer is doomed to failure because it represents a corrupted and deficient pattern of prayer from the original Language of Prayer. While simple prayer can give the soul relief and joy, it is merely mouthing words that provide hope and relief from despair. Simple prayer does not move mountains or initiate miracles. Let's examine simple prayer by observing what I call a standard style of praying. We may kneel or simply bow our heads and utter forth our heart felt desires. We pray to a higher spiritual being whom we feel can answer our prayers by divine grace. We may purify our selves before attempting this prayer by fasting or deep inner reflection. We voice the desires of our hearts and hope that God hears them and finds them acceptable so they will be answered. There is no assurance that God will hear those prayers. We wait and wonder why our prayers were not answered. Why was our prayer not empowered?

Most prayers offer requests for healing the sick as images of those who are sick fill the mind of those who offer forth the prayers. We pray for more money, better health, less problems in our lives and for some, they pray over every single thing they do. They have a prayer in their heart constantly. This form of prayer is the standard format taught in almost every Sunday School class today, but it lacks the empowerment to succeed. Let me tell you why.

The term prayer does not denote a religious application, but a spiritual law for achieving results. Spiritual laws transcend religious teachings. Religious teachings vary between sects, but a spiritual law does not transform according to belief. It does not require praise, honor or glory directed to a God any more than going out to your automobile and turning on the ignition. The ignition will start the automobile, regardless whether you heap praise, honor or glory to a God. Religion demands praise, honor and glory as tributes to a jealous deity who rules in all aspects of human affairs, but spiritual laws requires no praise, honor or glory.

The style and form of prayer taught today lacks the proprieties and proficiencies that will empower a transcendental moment, a shift in dimensional realities, replacing the old moment in time with a different moment in time. It can be likened to having three slides under a microscope. On one slide is a dark mark that shows up when all three slides are viewed together in the microscope. The Language of Prayer executes the protocols and techniques that metaphorically remove the slide with the dark mark resulting in the observer viewing only two slides with no dark mark showing up. It is that easy as removing the slide with the dark mark. First we will discuss the physics behind the Language of Prayer which is the science of quantum mechanics.

Our lives are composed of a pathway with infinite possibilities for future outcomes. We do not have to simply drift along the current, but we can take charge of our lives and become the Captain of our ship, directing the course we want to sail. We may choose the path we travel, we can replace one outcome with another and these transitions fall within the natural laws of quantum mechanics. We are not talking about anything supernatural or paranormal. Quantum mechanics or as it is sometimes called quantum weirdness, does fall within the laws of existing physics. We know so little of the subatomic realms that for most, it is mind boggling, but once the mind set is removed, the subatomic world can be fascinating.

We learn that according to the Observer Effect, the tiny electron revolving around the nucleus can only be observed for either momentum or for position, but not for both. The orbital path of the electron appears as a ghostly haze, the exact position is not determined until an observation is actually made. However when the observation is made, the observer is limited to either discovering the position or the trajectory, but not both.

To better understand this concept, consider a speeding bullet fired from a pistol can be freeze-framed to observe the physical location of the bullet, but the trajectory cannot be observed. However, if we use a slow motion camera, we can see the spinning bullet and observe its trajectory, but not its exact location. Thus, either one or the other can be observed, but not both. Here lies the foundation for understanding parallel dimensions and future outcomes.

There exist around us an infinite number of future outcomes or we could say an infinite number of parallel dimensions. We are in each of those dimensions, each one is a little different from our current realm. In one, I may have brown eyes instead of blue, or I may be tall and slim instead of short and chubby. The point is that each of these other dimensions, I exist as Dave Oester, but with minor differences. There will exist one dimension that would have my proverbial evil twin, but according to the models for Black Holes and Worm Holes, I would have to exceed the speed of light to access that dimension.

All of the other dimensions do not require the speed of light to gain access. We cannot initiate the shift to another dimension until we start the Observer Effect. When we focus on what we need, the parallel dimension will shift into alignment and replace the old with a different outcome. Have you caught the beauty of this prayer? Too many get hung up over the term prayer and fail to grasp the deeper spiritual law discussed. We say spiritual law, but we are really speaking of scientific law.

We are teaching a motif that allows a person to break out of a pattern that they no longer wish to retain and replace it with a new path that is more favorable to them. The Language of Prayer contains some lost ancient knowledge that had been recorded in the Dead Sea Scrolls that enable us to make those life changes we need. The Language of Prayer provides us with the techniques to change our future by replacing it with a different outcome, one of our choosing. The power is in each one of us to accomplish this task, if we only believe and follow the techniques. The choice is ours, we only have to believe.

The Language of Prayer could just as easily be called the Language of Blessing or the Language of Thanksgiving. The technique has nothing to do with religion or God, but is simply an application of existing natural laws. For example, when an apple falls from a tree, we do not say God pulled the apple down, but instead we use the apple as an example of the natural Law of Gravity at work. There exist many natural laws that we still do not understand the how's, but we know they work. The Language of Prayer is one such action that works in accordance with natural laws. Now we will examine the historic aspect of the Language of Prayer, outside the realm of quantum mechanics.

The Language of Prayer was being applied some five hundred years before the birth of the Jewish Jesus. The Language of Prayer was practiced at a remote desert Essene community of Qumran, along the Dead Sea, whose residents lived close to nature. The Essene Masters taught many principles that were later adopted and credited to Jesus. However, they originated from the ancient Hebrew text used by the Essenes known as the Dead Sea Scrolls.

Let's examine how the Language of Prayer was discovered. The scrolls were hidden in caves above the Dead Sea and discovered in 1947. The caves held many scrolls that contained fragmented text from the Hebrew Bible. Qumran was a desert community that practiced a spiritual way of life. Its members were called the Sons of Light and they lived according to the teachings of their Hebrew Bible. The knowledge and understanding found in the Dead Sea Scrolls became corrupted by the fourth century when the Council of Nicaea in AD 325 voted to remove books and text that were not supportive of the current philosophy held by the King. This man-made alteration forever corrupted the Language of Prayer so the Essene Masters sent copies of the scrolls to the four corners of earth to preserve the original text. Teachings from the Essene scrolls have been found in Tibet and in the American Southwest among some Native American tribes.

The Dead Sea Scrolls are important as they are the oldest text of the Hebrew Bible which covers the period between the end of the Old Testament and the beginning of the New Testament. This four hundred-year period of silence is an enigma because it appears to demonstrate that God stopped talking to prophets at the close of the Old Testament. This four hundred-year gap is not consistent with the teachings of the Old Testament, or else it seems to demonstrate that the Old Testament simply did not confirm God's dealings with man accurately. The good news is that the old Hebrew language has not changed in two thousand years so the text language in the Dead Sea Scrolls is still the Hebrew that is the language of the people. The Dead Sea Scrolls have not been translated and re-translated as have the many versions of the Bible.

In order to understand the full impact of the Language of Prayer, we must first understand some basic principles of Quantum Physics. Quantum theory suggests we will find the existence of many outcomes for a given moment in time. Rather than creating our reality, it may be more accurate to say that we build the circumstances into which we induce future outcomes, already established, into the focus of the here and now. These quantum principles validate the information that is presented in the Dead Sea Scrolls. Thanks to men like Bohr, Einstein, Wolfe and Hawkins, we have the understanding of quantum mechanics that enable us to understand the spiritual meaning found in the Dead Sea Scrolls.

The decisions made today will determine which quantum possibility will unfold for us in the future. quantum mechanics suggest that by redirecting our present focus, shifting our focus from the present to a new and different outcome, we compel the new course of events into our dimension while at the same time, we are dismissing our existing set of actions that are no longer desired by us. This is a very important concept that must not be overlooked. This is not a new concept because science fiction writers, such as Andre Norton and Fred Hoyle explored parallel dimensions and many worlds theories, back in the 1950s.

The future dimensions are determined by the decisions we make and actions we are taking today. The future is not set into stone, but it is mutable based on our behavior today. Change one decision today and future outcomes will be different. Our decisions become extremely important, let no one suggest that our individual decisions have no weight on what lies ahead. It has everything to do with the future.

The dimensional membrane between future realities, may be so thin that we fail to recognize it when we bridge over to a new dimensional outcome. We may feel that the choice has been spontaneous or natural, the change now allows us to experience a reality that was only a dream in the past. Our dimensional outcomes are another way of describing parallel dimensions that we are accessing into our existing dimensions. Prayer is the language that allows us to change future events within our lives. The Language of Prayer is like a transporter as seen on Star Trek, beaming one-dimensional reality into our dimensional reality.

For multiple outcomes to be considered implies that each reality is already created and present in our world. Perhaps in a form that we have yet to recognize, somewhere in creativity, as an embryonic mix of the physical and spiritual, each outcome in existence, but out of phase with our dimension, but available to shift into our dimension at any time. It may be that these alternate realities exist in parallel dimensions that are out of phase with our dimension. As our current outcome shifts away and the new outcome enters our dimension, for that briefest of nanoseconds, the two dimensions must coexist together. This overlapping of dimensions seems to occur most frequently when our dimension is subject to increased geomagnetic fields caused by the full and new moons or by solar flares and storms that bombard the earth with charged particles.

We have photographic evidence that we believe authenticates this moment in time when two dimensions coexist in our reality. Photographs that reveal the doppleganger like image of a second identical person in the photos. A second identical person, only this one is turned at a forty-five-degree angle and its body is transparent, almost like a double image. I said almost like a double image.

Today, Quantum Physics has validated this concept in the Bose-Einstein Condensate. This was named for the two men who predicted such an occurrence. What this means is that reality can occur during the time that two atoms occupy the same point, in the same space, at the same time. This concept has been observed and documented under laboratory conditions. Einstein said it was possible and photographic evidence suggests it is happening.

Quantum physics explains why parallel dimensions or many worlds are not only possible, but that they have existed since the beginning of time, at least since the Big Bang. We have all looked into mirrors that are facing each other and observed our reflections in each mirror continuing outward until they disappear into the far horizon. We wonder if each of those faces staring back at us are reflections or if they might be a window that is showing us our own face, each in a separate dimension removed from our own.

We know that quantum physics deals with minuscule objects, such as electrons, atoms and other subatomic particles. Such tiny objects cannot be observed with both position and momentum simultaneously. Whenever an observation occurs, the physical system undergoes a sudden change in its physical properties. Prior to the observation, the system is described by a combination of possible physical states, but after the observation, the system is no longer a combination of possible physical states, but is now a specific physical state. The other possible physical states simply vanish away. The observer has triggered the transformation. The Observer Effect is very important elements in parallel universes and parallel dimensions and is one of the keys to why the Language of Prayer is so effective at implementing dimensional shifts.

The Essene text suggests that the effect of prayer comes from something other than the words of the prayers themselves. The secret power lies beyond the spoken words, the incantations, and the rhythmic chants to the "powers that be." The Essences invite us to LIVE the intent of our petition in our lives. The secret power is found in a force that cannot be spoken or transmitted as the written word—the feeling or sensation that the words evoke with us.

It is the feeling or sensation of our invocations that open the door and lights our paths to the forces of the gods. To change the dimensional reality of our outer world, we must actually make the transformation of our desire from within. The Essene elders taught that we have three requirements to have a successful outcome. We must merge our thoughts and our emotions as one to create the feelings we need to become the silent language of nature. A simple equation would be: Feeling=Thoughts x Emotions. We must have the product of our thoughts and our emotions to create the feeling that is necessary to obtain a new outcome.

Yet, into this modern age of technology, we tend to ignore and dismiss our feelings, making them secondary to the focus on the physical world around us.

Simply speaking, prayer words have no power or effect. The calling upon a Deity or in the name of a Deity has no effect. This is why so many prayers fail to materialize. Often we offer up negative prayers, such as "please spare my son's life" or "please heal the cancer in my son's body." These are prayers that focus our attention on what we do not want. We envision our son laying in a hospital bed struggling for life or we see the tumor growing and overcoming the good cells in our boy's body when we pray. These prayers contain our visions of negative conditions, programming our prayers to fail. We actually get what we are praying for, but it is not a positive outcome, but the negative vision of doom that is fulfilled. The strength of our negative emotion, or fear consume us and our vision is more concentrated on the approaching death of our loved one. We want divine intervention to prevent it, but the subconscious still weakens our firm belief that the prayers will bring the outcome desired. We can speak holy words or call upon God, but our vision is still focused on the negative circumstances and it is those negative circumstances that are reinforced. When a Mother sobs and says, "I don't want to lose my baby," she has already succumbed to the loss.

We need to focus on a higher choice to bring change into our lives, and live from that prospective. Our focus must be on health and happiness, the positive features must be envisioned in our thoughts and feelings. We have to create a reality that is free of negative, but abundant with positive images. We must envision a state of condition that contains the sights, sounds and smells that match the reality we want as a replacement for the reality we no longer find acceptable. This different reality or dimension must become so real for us that we can see, feel and taste it. When this happens, that dimension will replace our existing dimension so the outcome will reflect the new dimension.

For example, instead of praying for sparing the life of the son, visualize the boy running in the field, climbing trees, playing baseball, laughing, joking and having fun. We must see the boy as the wind blows through his hair, must smell the apple he is bitting into and feel his happiness. This creates a different outcome, a feeling of life that you accept as reality. You must feel his aliveness, see him running and climbing and having fun as a boy ought to have. You focus on life, not on death and thus your prayers now take on power and life. You now envision life and health for the son, not laying ill in a hospital bed. The Language of Prayer is the key to life itself. It does not matter to what God you pray, but the important part is that you pray with intense feelings, your thoughts and emotions are merged as one in the feeling.

The Language of Prayer can be used by individuals of any faith because it does not rely upon a deity or a prescribed motif. The corrupted form of prayer has filtered down through the Christian sects as scholars failed to grasp the significance of what was being described, thereby corrupting the language further. Too many organized religions profess that prayer is the cornerstone of their faith, yet they lack the understanding for that cornerstone to be effective. It is not just the recitation of words that have power because the key is the role that feelings, emotions and thoughts are necessary to activate the secret power of the prayer.

The Essences taught about praying with all of your heart, might, mind and soul. The power is not in the words, but in the feelings or sensations within us. It is being able to change the outcome you do not want, to an outcome that is truly desired. There are no good or bad outcomes, only outcomes. Do not judge the outcome, accept them and learn from the lessons therein. We must take a Zen approach and not judge our outcomes, but simply realize that each one will teach us valuable lessons. If we no longer need the lesson, we can simply move onto another outcome with its new lessons. This nonjudgmental attitude is so important in so many different ways.

Gregg Braden describes in his book, *Isaiah Effect*, about the time he was invited to go with an Indian to perform a rain ceremony because of the terrible drought conditions that existed at the time. They drove to a site where a large medicine wheel was laid out in the earth. The Indian did a mediation to prepare himself and then took off his shoes and stood in the Medicine Wheel. He stepped into each of the four sections with his eyes closed and finally opened them and stepped out. He said he was done. Braden asked him if he wasn't going to do a rain dance or something as it did not take very long.

The Indian replied, "No. He was done." On the way back they chatted. The Indian explained, he prayed rain. He did not say he prayed for rain, but he prayed rain. He told Braden that he prayed what it was like to walk barefoot in the rain, to see the water laying on the ground after a hard rain, how their crops drank in the rain and grew tall. He told how it felt for him to be in the rain, how rain tasted as it fell into his open mouth and how it felt being soaked by the rain. He envisioned the rain, he felt the rain on his person and he believed the rain. He prayed with his heart, mind and soul. He did not express words, but he envisioned another outcome and accepted it as fact. His emotions, feelings and vision said it was rain falling on him, he felt the rain on his skin.

The Language of Prayer can be explained according to the quantum mechanics explanation of infinite dimensional outcomes or as we sometimes call them parallel dimensions. This concept is occasionally depicted as a parallel universe. Quantum mechanics have proven that two events can occupy the same space-time frame at the same time. This has led to developing an understanding about multiple outcomes. At any given moment in time, innumerable future possibilities exist. In one outcome a little boy lies ill in bed, but in a different future possible outcome, that boy is healthy and full of energy. All we do is replace one outcome with another that already exists. I know this sounds strange and may even resemble science fiction, but according to many scientists, including Albert Einstein, infinite future possibilities do exist at any given moment in our life.

The Language of Prayer would be considered the power in the magic used in the days of old by sorcerers and wizards. It enables spells, enchantments and the desires of our hearts to be manifested. In olden days, the power was said to come from the gods. Today we realize that the power comes from within us or the god within us, as we apply the Language of Prayer. This is one of the most important concepts of the new millennium because it can change our lives forever.

I think one of the hardest aspects to accept in this concept is that we have choices as to which path we can travel. We are not locked into a rut, barred from change. We have the freedom to change our lives to anything that we want, as long as we can visualize it, as long as we can emotionally taste it, and as long as we can believe it. I am not talking about having hope or desires, but of needs that MUST be fulfilled. We may desire many things, but that does not mean we are motivated to the point of needing it. We may desire a million dollars, but we also believe that it is impossible to happen. We limit ourselves and bind ourselves to the humanness that has been pounded into our heads from the onset of our understanding, therefore the Language of Prayer is elusive to us. We don't stray outside the limits set for us by church doctrines, our thinking limits the God-given abilities that we have deep within each one of us. One of those abilities is the effective use of the

Language of Prayer and the ability to effect dramatic change in our lives.

Magic is simply learning how to access an alternative reality that coexists with us. The concept of parallel dimensions may have been science fiction a decade ago, but today we know that other dimensions exist along side our dimension. Magic is the bridge that allows us to leap into another dimension, replacing our old dimension with a new reality and a new outcome that is more favorable to our goals or needs. We can open the dimensional portal by applying the techniques and directing forth the energy necessary to activate the transformation. In ancient days, wizards and sages understood this energy and today by Quantum Physics, we can understand the scientific explanation as to this transformational process.

We have before us the opportunity to change our lives anyway we need to. If the pathway we travel is one that we do not want to be on, we can change it by envisioning a new path, complete with what we need. We are only limited by our beliefs and our lack of understanding. Parallel dimensions do exist and the fabric of time and space can be bent, allowing parallel dimensions to overlap into our own reality.

The concept of parallel dimensions may be something as simple as imagining a radio with a big tuning dial. As we turn the dial, we are receiving different frequencies, all coexisting together, each in their own slot, so to speak. The Magic of the Language of Prayer can be likened to this radio set. We simply switch to another frequency, thereby, replacing the old dimension with a new dimension that only affects us and not the world around us.

We may have an infinite number of dimensions existing all around us and all we have to do is learn how to dial into the station we want. Just as the electromagnetic spectrum goes from 0 hertz to infinity. Certain frequencies represent the visual light range and still higher frequencies may represent infrared or ultraviolet frequencies. Why is it difficult to imagine that dimensional frequencies also exist and that they can be accessed by tuning into the right frequencies? Focus, concentration, visualization and imaging acts as the tuner for us to access these dimensional frequencies.

Concentration, Focus, Mediation and Imaging

The Language of Prayer is one method that can effectively modify or alter future outcomes, but not everyone may be able to apply this technique to achieve their desired outcome. We have included an alternate method of achieving the same results that employs symbolism, rituals and chants to accomplish the same results as the Language of Prayer. Both methods require concentration, focus, mediation and imaging to achieve the desired results.

Magic denotes the projection of natural energies to produce needed effects of our choosing. Therefore, to begin the practice of magic, one must learn certain basic techniques: concentration, focusing, meditation and imaging. The purpose of learning these techniques is two fold. The primary reason is to aid you in learning to center yourself and to remove the stress and tension of your busy days. The second reason is to aid you in developing the skills to effectively visualize, focus and concentrate on your magic. Magic will not work if you are unable to remove the scattered thoughts that constantly flow into our minds. We must learn to control and limit random thoughts from cascading into our minds while we are engaged in magic. The following techniques will provide some exercises to develop the skills necessary for the working of magic and to help you become centered and grounded.

Concentration is holding an image or thought in your mind without interruption. Concentration is of prime importance during actual rituals when everything not directly related to what you are doing must be excluded from your thoughts. You must be so absorbed in your ritual and why you are doing it that no unrelated noise, no thoughts of the day's happenings, not even the doorbell or even the telephone, are allowed to disrupt your focus.

Focusing is adjusting your "inner eye" on a particular object or goal. It is different from concentration, yet is an integral part of it. Focusing your "inner eye," on a goal aids you to visualize the objective more clearly.

Visualization is absolutely necessary and when combined with emotion and determination, is essential to unlock the right brain, to start the process which fulfills your desires. Focusing and concentrating on what you are doing in ritual conveys your mind's power and energies into the activity, strengthening and making it a reality.

In the practice of meditation, you use your powers of focusing, concentration, imaging, and relaxation to center yourself, control destructive emotions, and gain insight. Meditation also brings a heightened sense of awareness and increased ability to visualize. Meditation calms the soul and allows one to become intune to the natural vibrations of the earth which according to Nikola Tesla resonates at 7.82 hertz. This allows your brain wave to also resonate at the same frequency, as if two hearts are beating as one.

One technique to developing good concentration is to use a candle and its flame. Stare at the flame for a minute and than close your eyes and concentration on seeing the flame in front of you. The longer you can hold that image the better you will become. Many people lose the image almost immediately. This is normal. Concentration takes practice and work. Continue this exercise until you are able to retain the image of the flame in your mind. Other objects can be used to practice with during the day. If you are taking a walk, stop and stare at an object and close your eyes. See that object and hold its image as long as you can. At work, concentrate on a fixed object and hold the image as long as possible. This technique can be practiced at night before going to sleep. Put a picture on the wall and stare at it and then close your eyes and hold the image in your mind as long as possible. When you feel that you can accomplish this "holding the image' in your mind, you are ready to move onto Focusing.

Focusing is related to Concentration, but now you to focus on details of the image you are holding into your mind. In your mind's eye, you zoom in on the object and see the details as you hold the image in your mind. This technique can be practice anywhere, at home, at the office or while taking a walk. You can practice this technique at bedtime, before retiring for the night. Focus on your object and close your eyes and see the details as if you zoomed in on it. Hold the detailed image in your mind as long as possible.

Meditation is different from prayer. In meditation the purpose is to rid your body of stress and tension and to become intune with the energies around you. One of the first things you will need to do is find a quiet area where you will not be disturbed. Be sure the telephone is either turned off or unplugged from the wall so you will not hear that annoying ring while you are doing the meditation.

There are many ways to do meditations. We are suggesting one way that has worked for us. Find a comfortable chair with a straight back. If this is not comfortable, perhaps lay down and do not cross your legs or arms. Imagine a giant roller is moving from your head down to your ankles. The roller is pushing stress and tension away from you as it exits the feet. Once you feel all tension and stress gone, take several deep breaths and hold them for a second or two and slow let out the air. Take another deep breath slowly, hold it and then release it slowly. Imagine you are on an elevator with the floor numbers showing. Slowly descend from ten to one and each time you descend a floor, focus on being relaxed and at peace. Imagine when you reach the bottom that you are very relaxed and at peace. Focus on hearing your own heart beating. Listen to your own heart beat and know that you are completely relaxed and at peace with yourself and with nature around you.

It is during this time of mediation that you will be open to the powers that be, new thoughts may flow into your mind. Listen for guidance that may come to you. Focus on questions you have and allow the energies of nature to provide the guidance back to you. This is also the time that you practice your projection, visualize yourself somewhere else. You may want to have a secret place that you go to when you need to be alone. Some have pictured a garden, others a pastoral setting, still others may have a secret cave that is secure and comfortable. Whatever safe place you pick, this will become you secret place that you can visit whenever you do meditations.

You are accessing the magical energy while you are in meditation. This Force is both subtle and at the same time extremely strong. At first you may not realize that you are using the Force as you project yourself. Visualize the place you want to be and than focus all your energy into that thought. Do not allow outside thoughts to take root, allow them to enter and pass through the window of your mind. If you have a hard time visualizing the Force, imagine heat waves coming off of the desert floor at noon. I am sure that you have seen with your eyes those shimmering heat waves on a highway during the summer. The *Force* is like the shimmering energy raising above the highway. The closer you get, the shimmering waves still appear to be in the distance, yet you have traveled much closer, yet the waves never get closer. The magical energy is always in and around us, we can never leave it behind and travel without it.

The mechanism that triggers the magical energy is initiated by deceiving the left analytical brain while the right creative brain interprets the symbolic instructions and forwards the new commands to the subconscious that acts upon the new set of instructions without bias. For example, if I want to visualize wealth, I would find a photograph of an oil well and use it to visualize the oil well horsehead pumping up and down, as dollar signs flow into the holding tanks. Black symbolizes wealth to me because a few years ago, I owned an oil and gas drilling company. The crude oil was black in color and was nicknamed Black Gold. Even in my dreams, black represents money, wealth or income.

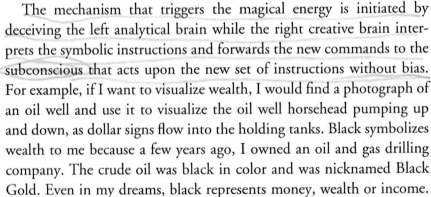

The important point is to use symbols that are important to you so the right brain will understand the instructions.

Once you have gained a comfort zone with these simply and basic techniques, you are ready to progress to the next level. Again, for magic to work, you have to believe that it will work. The power to work the magic is already within you, all we are doing is reminding you of how to use that magic. Magic is not good or bad, but it is much like a loaded handgunl. Guns don't kill people, people kill people. The handgun is neutral, how the handgun is used is up to you. Think of magic in terms of quantum physics, the science that explains parallel dimensions. Your future is mutable, by that we mean that your future is not set in stone. If it was, you could never change it, bu the future is not set in stone. It exists only as possibilities as this point. Until the possibilities become reality, it is still alterable and therefore mutable. Magic is choosing the possibilities you want to exist within your dimension.

We got an email from a lady who was diagnosed with cancer. She has a five-year-old daughter and does not know how to prepare her for her death. Now lets looks at this sad event in a different light. In one dimension she is diagnosed with cancer and will probably die. In another dimension that is coexisting with her is a dimension where she is not diagnosed with cancer. If she will replace the current dimension with the alternative dimension where she does not have cancer, it will merge into her existing dimension as a seamless transition. She will not even know it has happened until she returns to the doctor and he or she is shocked as there is no sign of the cancer. The doctor may say it is a miracle, but it was the Language of Prayer in operation. You have to believe in magic for magic to work for you and the transcendental experience will be like magic is what science. There are endless future possibilities that exist at any give moment in our life. We choose the future possibility we want in our life and than we draw that reality to us by the techniques.

The Importance of Meditation

We can experience the realm beyond without having a Near-death Experience. We can access the realm beyond through meditation. Meditation provides an easy method to rise beyond the body naturally and comfortably. People can make this connection with the inner Light. We don't have to pass from this physical life into death, to accomplish this.

Mystics and saints of various religions provide us with numerous references to the inner Light. Descriptions of divine Light and of heavenly realms are given in the Bible. Christ said, "If thine eyes be single, thy whole body shall be full of Light." (Matthew 6:22)

In speaking of the inner light and sound, Saint Rajinder Singh, great saint and master of meditation say, "The aspirant sees the real Light within him, where normally the inner eye is covered by a thick veil of darkness. He then realizes that the tradition of the lighted candle found in churches and temples are to remind him of the divine Light of Heaven within. This Light grows to the radiance of several suns put together as he advances on the way. He understands that the unceasing internal Sound he contacts within is the Divine Link called, 'word', by Christ, 'Kalma and Nida-I-Asmani' in the Koran, 'and' in the Vedas, 'Udgit' in the Upanishads, 'sraosha' by the Zorastrians, and 'Naam' and 'Shahd' by the saints and masters."

In the 15th century, in India, meditation was taught as a science by such great saints as Guru Nanak and Kabir Sahib. Meditation can be taught as a science to anyone, irrespective of religious backgrounds. The purpose is so people can rise above their bodies to seek the spiritual realms to experience the peace, joy and bliss for themselves.

This meditation experience is described in the same ways as those describing Near-death Experiences. Both involve the entering into a world of pure Light. In Near-death Experiences, people are just entering into the threshold of the spirit world, they are then returned to their physical bodies. People who meditate cross the threshold of the spirit realm to explore inner regions. In Near-death Experiences, as in meditation can explore further to find brighter light and more ethereal realms.

Kabair and Saomi Ji Maharaji have explored inner realms, describing varying bright Lights. They also describe hearing an "inner celestial music." There are different planes created by the flow of Light and music from God. "There is a supracausal plane that contains a predominance of spirit and a thin veil of illusion. Then there is a region in which there are equal parts spirit and matter known as the causal plane. The astral plane contains more matter and less of spirit. Thus, the density of matter increased as the current flowed farther from God."

Mainstream religion teaches us that when the physical body dies, the soul departs. We know that the soul is not made up of matter, but is an ethereal substance, unlike the physical body. A person returning from an NDE, describes having a body of Light. In this physical plane, we cannot see these bodies of Light. They are beyond our ability to see, being on a plane of a different vibrational rate and into a realm closer to what we know as the infrared range.

Kabair and Saomi Ji Maharaji said, "The mechanics of the meditation process are that of connecting the soul within us with the current of Light and Sound as a method of traveling out of the physical body. When this connection occurs, we can then merge and travel with it to the higher, spiritual realms."

We identify ourselves so fully by our body and our mind, we have forgotten the essence of who we are. We focus on the physical appearance most of all that defines who we are. Even our mind, our intelligence has become secondary to the importance of what we look like. Yet the soul, the essence and energy of whom we are, is the same essence as God. God of All, is love, joy and peace. We need to seek these things which are our true nature that fill us with bliss. By identifying ourselves with our soul, we can experience divine Light and the love within ourselves.

Our soul cannot enter into the spiritual realms until it is freed of all negative thought. Meditation requires full concentrated focus, without negative interference. With the knowledge we gain of what lies beyond this physical life, we can give comfort and strength to those around us.

A Meditation Technique

Meditation is a technique by which deep stillness and attention is focused to the very source of thought. By tuning out the outer world, we tune into the depth of our inner self to access a higher consciousness. It is a discipline of the mind and body as a means to strengthen our self awareness and spirituality.

Meditation is a powerful tool for spiritual and personal growth, opening our minds to a greater understanding of life and our relationship to life. We understand life by our experiences. Being human, our predisposed religious beliefs and society and its attitudes regarding death, block our awareness and our true comprehension of death and beyond. To most all of humanity, death remains a great mystery. We may only know the absolute truth when we experience it ourselves. Meanwhile, we can imagine, read information being published and theorize what the experience will be like.

We consciously leave our physical bodies every night in sleep, traveling to to alternate dimensions or to the astral plane or perhaps, being the closest thing to death we experience now. Meditation is practiced along the same principles, during a waking state, relaxing the body and mind to experience a more focused, dreamlike state.

Meditation should be a part of a persons daily routine. Like anything else we do, the more it is practiced the more perfected we can become at Meditation. It should always be practiced in a place where there will be no outside distractions. Everything involves awareness of what you focus on.

To begin, find a comfortable place to sit, back straight and feet flat on the floor to align the chakras. This will enable you to receive higher vibrations. Be aware of your body, focus on your deep breathing, bringing in the good air, exhaling the old, stale air in the lungs. Envision your body filling with earth energies, feeling centered and grounded.

Visualize a powerful white light coming down into your head, surrounding and energizing. It penetrates and re-energizes throughout your body. Clear your mind of outside thought and feelings removing the energy of others from you. Imagine a vacuum cleaner, suctioning away the negative, burdensome thoughts and feelings until you feel lighter, happier and freer. Now envision a pure white, protective light surrounding you. Your mind should be receptive and aware.

To find the light of life within you, visualize a garden filled with the beauty of the flowers of your choosing. Take in the beauty surrounding you. In the garden also stands a mirror. Walk to the mirror and look at the image reflected back to you. See your face and body as they are now in as much detail as you can.

Staring at yourself in the mirror, focus on the expectations others have of you. See the areas that need forgiveness and situations for which you feel guilty. Bring love into the image with the people and situations. Envision the light of love emanating from your heart touching everyone and everything. Let that light of love touch and surround you also.

Step away from the mirror and envision once again, the garden with its large, brightly colored flowers, green grass, blue sky and warm sunlight. Your awareness is of the loving spiritual entity you are.

This is one example of a very simple Meditation that can aid in improving the way that a person feels about themselves. The more a person can practice Meditational skills that are flooded with positive love and forgiveness, the better the outside world looks and the happier that person becomes. It is not only the Meditation but the influence of positive energy that strengthens us to endure any hardship.

Our thoughts, our attitudes and our emotions are all forms of energy, constantly influencing the world around us. Physicists no long consider themselves detached observers. They know their very presence influences the properties of the particle/waves they study. Our attitudes affect the cycles within and around us. Aware of this, the Tao people live consciously, respectfully, knowing they exert a powerful influence on their world. Most people are unaware of this even though it has been proven scientifically.

Not only do we influence people around us; we are continually affected by the actions and attitudes of others. Spending time with other people means breathing the same air, sharing the same energy field. Some interaction is energizing. Others deplete us, draining our energy which we can feel, clearly and distinctly. Being exhausted after being together with someone, the person is draining your energy. Unbalanced, uncentered, out of touch with the source of "chi" in their lives, such people subsist on energy transfusions from others. These people are emotional vampires.

Emotional vampires are always clamoring for help. Whenever something goes wrong, they run to a strong friend to rescue them, acting so helpless that others feel guilty refusing to listen. Attaching themselves like barnacles, these people become increasingly demanding and dependent. They do not have the abilities to deal with problems in their lives, so this dumping process is a habit in which they circumvent taking responsibility for themselves.

People who have low self-esteem often get caught up in the negative energies of others. Their insecurity and confusion makes them vulnerable to manipulators and emotional vampires.

We can transcend hostile cycles in our personal lives-in relationships, health, careers, and finances. We can also overcome hostile cycles in society. Whether these cycles are great or small, personal or universal, the way to transcend them is by centering, nonresistance and taking positive action. When a person can keep themselves centered and in balance, they have the ability to endure whatever comes to them.

Succumbing to fear or guilt only empowers manipulators who draw us into negativity. We give what inevitably comes back to us. Negativity begets negativity. Nonresistance neutralizes negative cycles. When our heart and minds are no longer troubled by negative emotions, we can act wisely, defusing negativity with wisdom of the Tao. Nonresistance helps us shift from negative to positive. When no one overreacts, the hostile cycle winds down.

Resisting change leads to depression, emotional drain and exhaustion. Positive action rebuilds self-esteem. Maintaining a standard of order is positive action, breaking the negative cycle. The first law of the universe is order, and we need to respect the natural order within and around us.

Our physical bodies do not become strong unless we put the necessary nutrients into them. Our spiritual-self does not progress without proper care either. We grow as we increase in knowledge. Some growth is easy and painless, but some comes only after trial and tears. The easy, painless changes, as in our behavior, are surface changes. Major changes are a result of harsh, life-changing events. These are the essential, deep, spiritual changes, with deeper meaning and purpose.

Passage to the Subconscious

Our mind operates at four different mental levels depending on the needs of the body. These four levels follow a natural cycle from one level to another. We move from full consciousness and awareness (beta) to subconscious state (alpha) to a light sleep (theta) and to a deep sleep state (delta). The cycle is repeated when we awake going from the delta to theta to alpha to beta. The four levels represent patterns of brain waves represents the natural rhythm or cadence. The brain is influenced by both internal and external sources that can effect changes to these rhythms or cadences...

In our most active state, the *Beta*, we are fully awake and active. This is the level of mental activity that we experience each and every day. This is our wide awake, fully alert mind that we use for our daily functions, such as driving our vehicle, working on the computer, working in the garden going shopping for food. The beta level employs about 75% toward those life-controlling functions and only about 25% toward concentrated conscious thought. The brain wave frequencies are generally around 35 hertz. Hertz is the scientific name for cycles. When we say 35 hertz, we are saying that it vibrates 35 times a second.

The *Alpha* level may be referred to as our subconscious mind, entered into by such activities as biofeedback, mediation and daydreaming. Alpha has nearly 100% concentration compared to beta's 25% concentration level. Alpha level is the calm and related state that is most desirable for programming or reprogramming of our subconscious mind and is the end goal for those who practice mediation.

Alpha brain waves are in the 7 to 11 hertz which means it is vibrating at 7 to 11 times a second. It is interesting that the Schumann Resonance frequency for the earth is considered to be 7.82 hertz. The natural occurring frequency of 7.82 hertz suggest that the earth is vibrating at the same frequency as the brain's Alpha level. When we do mediation we learn to lower the rhythm of our brain from the beta level down to the alpha brain wave frequency, thus we can become at one with the earth. This process has been called At-One-Ment. If we want to draw energy from Mother Earth, we do so by coming into harmony with the frequency of the earth or we could say, at resonance with the earth.

This frequency can also be induced by artificial means, such as a signal generator or an ELF emitter built around the 555 IC chip. I have built many of the so called, "stress relaxers" based on the 555 IC chip and tuned to the 8-hertz range. This frequency induces a state of relaxation and remove stress which cannot exist at that frequency range.

The *Theta* level is that part of the unaware and unawake mind that functions in light sleep. This is the stage of sleep when we first drift off and precedes the deeper delta levels. The brain wave frequency range for theta is generally between 3 and 6 hertz.

The *Delta* level is deepest level of sleep and where the greatest rest is obtained and is the place for healing of the body. This is characteristic of brain waves in the .5 hertz range. This frequency range is also used in sport medicine for healing of tissues by trainers. Several patents are issued with the devices operating in the .5 hertz range.

The ideal state for accessing the subconscious mind is the alpha level, with the brain waves operating at about 8 hertz. This is the optimum condition for receiving input into the subconscious mind. If this brain wave frequency can be achieved than all programming directed into the subconscious mind will be achieved without delay. This frequency is achieved in ritualistic pagan ceremonies by drumming, dancing, chanting and singing. The flickering flames of a fire contrasted against the darkness of the night can act as a strobe light affecting our conscious minds. The frequency of the drumming can also establishes the cadence that is needed to entrain the brain. The rhyme of a chant can induce an alpha state. Why is the rhyme and frequency important in establishing a cadence?

Research has found that the brain waves can be lowered to coincide with an external source of beat or cadence. Just as within a clock shop, all clocks will chime together, we say that this process of coming into harmony with an external cadence is entrainment. This is the principle behind mediation, we can learn to lower our brain waves and is taught in biofeedback classes for those who must learn to slow down and take control of their lives.

One of the fastest techniques for achieving this 8-hertz alpha level is one that I learned a long time ago. It is easy to do and can put you in the proper brain wave pattern in just seconds. The more this technique is practiced, the faster the subconscious mind can be accessed when the spells, chants and enchantments are done.

First establish an imaginary circle of protection around yourself. This can be done by imagining a sphere of white light surrounding everything with this circle of protection. Feel the energy that is surrounding and protecting every thing within the circle. You are now protected from outside negative energy fields. Now begin the Twenty-to-One Approach.

The Twenty-to-One approach begins by closing your eyes and clearing your mind of the daily clutter. Our mind must be stilled and silenced. This is difficult when first starting out. Random thoughts jump at the chance to enter our minds. Do not think of anything. Do not allow any thoughts to remain. If a stray thought enters your mind, allow it to depart without grabbing hold of it. If you should grab hold to the thought, you must start your timer over and begin again.

Once your mind is clear of all thoughts, imagine a digital readout on a timer whose numbers descends from twenty to one. In your mind's eye watch the digital display of each number starting at 20 and descending to 1. Imagine seeing each number in your mind and mentally watch the numbers descend. Do not allow random thoughts to dwell within your mind, let them pass on through. When you get to one, your brain wave will be in the alpha range and your subconscious mind is fully open to programming.

If at any time a stray thought enters the mind and lingers, you must start over from 20 and descend once again. It is important to start over because when you dwell on a thought, your mind returns to fully alert at the beta level. When this happens, you have to repeat the exercise, else your brain waves remain at the beta level and your subconscious mind is closed down for inputting your desired objectives.

Once you are arrived at one without any stray thoughts lingering with you, start your own ceremony or ritual. Chants the ritual spell, focus on the words, feel the energy of the emotions, see the outcome you are seeking.

Creation of Spells and
Enchantments

The beauty of the *Magic Dimensions* is that you can create your own chants and spells. The power of the spell or chant is not in the words your create, but the feelings and emotions of the words that empower the transcendental happening. This is a very important concept in the art of magic. It is not the words, but the feelings and emotions generated by the words that have an effect. Spells or chants should be simple to say and simple to understand. Anyone can create a spell or chant because it comes from the heart and is focused toward a needed objective. In a way, chants and spells are like poems, some may rhyme and some may not. This is your opportunity to customize a chant or spell to your own disposition. No one is going to judge the chant or spell, so you can be really creative or very simple and direct.

Spells are dime a dozen, every book on witchcraft, shamanism or pagan ceremonies will have spells and chants listed. One spell is not better than another, one has no more power than another. The older the spell does not mean it is more powerful. There is no set standard for spells or the deities they hail. Some spells invoke the male and female energies, some call upon the gods and goddess or invoke mythological entities. Some spells will invoke the saints of Christendom while still others simply call upon the energies of Mother Nature. The Gnostic Christian spells used imperishable names and natural plants and flowers.

Ancient Christian Magic relates a spell used by Jesus for ascending through the heavens. This Gnostic spell was invoked by Jesus to his disciples during a baptism by fire ceremony. This spell called for incense to be burned as the disciples stood in a circle with their feet touching each other. Jesus crowned each disciple with pigeon grass, put the plant doghead into their mouth, knotgrass under their feet and had each hold a pebble with the number seven in their two hands along with chrysanthemum. Jesus than invoked the imperishable names that are in the treasury of the light after speaking a lengthy oration, similar to the manner used by King Solomon in the *Keys of Solomon*. It is interesting that this spell allowed his disciples to ascend through the various levels to get to heaven. Sounds a lot like the concept of parallel dimensions or ascending through dimensions until the one you seek is found.

It does not matter if your spell invokes divine entities, imperishable names or simply call upon the energies of the Universe, because you choose what has meaning to you in your life. You choose the deity or mythological figures that has meaning to you. It is the idea that duality and balance can be found in all things that form the basis for practitioners to call upon the male and female energies, or the god and goddess energies. It is not the names that are important, but it is the feelings and emotions that are evoked. This is one of the primary lessons learned from our study of the *Keys of Solomon* where the Hebrew characters have a mystical context beyond just being a part of the alphabet. The Hebrew letters represent mystical concepts that are taught in Qabbalistical Magic.

In witchcraft, the Book of Shadows is your own private journal of spells that work for you. This book can contain your notes, special combination of herbs for healing and your private feelings about them. There is nothing sacred about a Book of Shadows. No two Books of Shadows are the same because no two practitioners are the same. There is no right spell and no wrong spell, except when it comes to the purpose of creating the spell. One Book of Shadows is not better than another nor are the old Book of Shadows more powerful than the ones created today. Consider the Book of Shadows as your private diary where you write your inner thoughts, recipe for spells that work for you and chants that have worked successfully. This is your cookbook of life.

If someone wanted to create a curse, the steps would be the same. Another name for spell is hex which can be positive or negative. The only difference goes back to the person creating the spell, chant, hex or enchantment. A good example, the Christian sect known as the Amish people paint huge hex symbols on their barns for protection. The Wicca Rede says do what you want, but harm none. This bit of advise is well spoken. Magic should never be used for negative purposes. Remember, what goes around will come around. We will reap what we sow, so be aware that your actions will be the same actions coming back to haunt you.

However, one can accomplish much without harming others. For example, instead of doing a spell to hurt someone, why not do a spell that causes them to move from the area. Thus, your end results would be the same, but the latter method would not harm them. Those who endorse reincarnation would suggest that any negative acts will harm you in the end because you will have karma to deal with, and most practitioners want to be adding positive to the karma balance. Always explore your options and use common sense before you undertake a spell or chant. Explore the ramifications and decide on the best course of actions. Never do anything in anger, but do it in love. Magic is not for a child to play parlor games with, but must be used wisely and with discretion, else repercussions will befall the practitioner.

I like to create my spells, chants and enchantments tailored to what I want them to accomplish. I work on them for days at a time, each time tweaking them so they sound more like what I feel they should. Perform some dry runs, how do they sound? How do they feel? If something doesn't sound just right, continue working on them until you feel good about them. Be careful that you harm none or cause yourself to be harmed by the spell. I think of the spells more as affirmations of what I want to accomplish. Do not be threatened by the label, be it spells or affirmation, the end results will be the same.

This may create a series of life events that are better or worse, so you have still intervened in their karmic path

The spell, chant or enchantment is nothing more than a combination of words that helps you to focus on the objective you are seeking. It has no magical powers in and of itself. The chant, spell or enchantment are simply words in verse form. The power comes from within you and from the energies of nature to empower the focus and concentration. When the *force* is accessed, the power to animate the focused concentration is in progress. Repeat the spell over and over. Each time increasing the tempo while building momentum and emotions until you feel you have reached the zenith and than focus that release of energy outward.

Most often the beginner starts out with some basic spells, chants and enchantment that covers life's basic issues, such as attracting money, healing sickness, repelling negative energy and personal travel protections for those hectic days driving to and from work. Examples of these kinds of spells will be provided so you can see how simple they are to create. Nothing is sacred when it comes to creating spells, no special language, no special names for Deity or special religious tag.

You can create your verse according to your personal inspiration. Those deeply interested in shamanism can create verses around animal totems and the common terminology associated with Native American ceremonies. Those involved with witchcraft or Wicca may use the Lord and Lady or the god and goddess with the verse to give it meaning to them.

Setting a proper environment so the mind can better focus on the objective can be aided by the use of incense, smudge sticks and scented burn sticks. We have visited shops that sell incense and scented burn sticks, only to be turned away by the strong aroma present in those shops. Always be careful of what incense is being used, as some of them may induce headaches because the fragrance is too strong. Choose scents that promote the spiritual conditions you are establishing. Scents, such as sage are burned in cleansing or purification ceremonies. Choose an incense that matches the ceremony you are doing. How do you know which is the best? Experiment with them, if the fragrance is distracting, avoid its use. If it enable you to transcend the moment, consider adding it to your list of incense to use. Some people benefit from the burning of scented wood, while others find it distracting. The decision is up to you, if it does not feel right, disregard it.

Do not be afraid to pen verses, no one is going to grade them or even see them. The verses are for your private benefit and hopefully will enable you to focus and concentrate on the words as they are chanted. These verse work best if kept in a simple state, avoid large and complex words as they become a distraction to you when they are chanted.

You can have a spell for all occasions or you can create a selective number of spells that are for specific purposes. This is the fun part of working with magic. This is the outward ritual that you will be conducting while at the same time inaugurating the spiritual fulfillment of your objective. This is the yin yang balance that is so important in nature.

If you are having problems at this stage of creating spells or accepting magic, take some time out and read a Harry Potter book and feel the magic that he is living. I am very impressed with this series of books and recommend them fully to anyone who wants to understand more about magic. The books do not teach you about how to work magic, but of living with magic. Sometimes we have to break out of our mind set and allow our mind to see the other side of the coin. As I have said time and again, magic works if you believe it will work.

Samples of Spells and Chants

The following samples of spells are taken from my own collection of spells, or as witches say, the Book of Shadow. These spells, chants and enchantments were created by us for our specific needs and can be adapted to your situation by simply substituting replacement words or terms of your creation. The important point is that while you are saying the chant or spell, focus, concentrate and imagine seeing the outcome you are seeking.

The better you can visualize the outcome, empowered by your feelings and emotions, the faster the energy peak will be achieved. The use of drums, rattles or other music instruments by another or by listening to same on a CD or music tape will aid in the entrainment of the brain waves to lower to the alpha state that allows direct access for the focusing, concentration or visualization of your objective.

Remember all of the chanting, drums, rattles or other music sources are simply devices that will capture the attention of the left brain and keep it busy with the physical trappings as the right brain is programed by the symbols of the chant or spell.

CONSECRATE THE SACRED CIRCLE

We do not draw a nine-foot circle on the ground for our ceremonies, nor do we practice the Wicca style of the circle ceremony. This is not to suggest that their style and method is wrong, but it does not appeal to us so we have developed a style that we are comfortable with. This is the advantage of understanding magic, it is not the rituals, but the feelings and emotions that are the focal point of magic. We simply create a sphere of white light that will protect us from negative energies while

the doorway is opened to other realms. The following enchantment
should be of benefit.

While saying these words, imagine with your mind's eye, a blue circle of energy that becomes a sphere of white light that encompasses the
circle in a dome shaped energy field. This dome shaped energy field
might be considered a force field that prevents negative energy from
penetrating. The Star War program was suppose to pattern such a
energy shield based on Nikola Testa's designs. This energy shield
would protect anything within it from outside energy probes.

> I consecrate this sacred circle of energy,
> Open a sphere of white light to protect,
> All negative vibrations vanish within.
> I invite my friends and spirit guide to join,
> As I start my magic journey.

BLESSING CHANT

Many cultures suggest a purification ceremony before the working of
magic. The purification ritual would prepare us for working with the
sacred energies that many believe come from the gods. Once such purification chant is what we call a Blessing Chant. This chant is also excellent to do when you are feeling down and want to recommit yourself to
following your path in life. If you prefer to use other names than all
you have to do is substitute them for the ones we have used.

> In this place of power, I open myself,
> In this place and in this time I give thanks.
> As I seek bounties from thy hand,
> I open myself to your divine Essence.
> May I see the divine in nature,
> nature in the divine and
> divine within myself and all else.

Oh Great Spirit who guides us all,
I beseech thy bounties both above and below.

SPELL TO REPEL NEGATIVE ENERGY

This spell is best done on a waning moon (After full moon to the new moon) or on the new moon. It is designed to repel negative energy that has been directed to you and return it to the source even stronger than before. This spell can be repeated over and over as you add emotion and feelings to the words. When you feel that the energy has peaked, you can either direct the energy into a candle that will release this spell as it burns, or discharge it outward as in a cone of energy. The cone shape comes from the circular pattern that narrows at the top as in a funnel. The small end is the broadcast end that transmits the energized spell. The important point is that while you are saying the chant or spell, focus, concentrate and imagine seeing the outcome you are seeking. The better you can visualize the outcome, empowered by your feelings and emotions, the faster the energy peak will be achieved.

I enter this magical realm,
Where spells and charms are real.
By quantum physics or wizard chants,
empower this spell I now enchant
I create this spell for repelling negative.
I call forth energies from above and below,
Send all negative back to its source.

I call forth the energies of Air,
Carry back this foul energy on Raven's wings.
I call forth the energies of Fire,
Give my spell the blazing energy to repeal.
I call forth the energies of Water,
Make my spell like raging waters.

I call forth the energies of Earth,
Give my spell force and power.

Whether you be born of thought or deed,
Return now to those that sent you!
Become three fold stronger as you fly,
Let them experience what they impart.
Begone foul troublemakers now depart,
Fly back to the source I now command.
Leave this place as you found it,
Free of evil and filled with love.

When the emotional peak has been reached, you have the option of sending the spell forth with the following words.

Now I send this spell forth,
Make it so, so mote it be!

Or you can charge a white candle with this highly energized spell so when the candle burns, the energy is released.

I now charged this White candle,
As it burns, empower the spell.

While the White candle has no power to grant as it is only wax. The burning candle reminds us to focus of our objective and to keep it foremost in our minds. We visualize the energy being released which is the important aspect to a burning candle.

SPELL FOR PROTECTION FROM TERRORIST ATTACK

Since the terrible and cowardly attack by terrorists sent by Osama Bin Laden on September 11, 2001 against the people of New York City, have many concerned with additional terrorist attacks. This spell is derived from the spell, To Repel Negative Energy and is modified for protection against terrorist attacks. Notice how easy it is to adapt spells to specific needs. This spell is best done on a waning moon (After full moon to the new moon) or on the new moon. It is designed to repel negative energy that has been directed to you and return it to the source even stronger than before. This spell can be repeated over and over as you add emotion and feelings to the words. When you feel that the energy has peaked, you can either direct the energy into a candle that will release this spell as it burns, or discharge it outward as in a cone of energy. The cone shape comes from the circular pattern that narrows at the top as in a funnel. The small end is the broadcast end that transmits the energized spell. The important point is that while you are saying the chant or spell, focus, concentrate and imagine seeing the outcome you are seeking. The better you can visualize the outcome, empowered by your feelings and emotions, the faster the energy peak will be achieved.

> *I enter this magical realm,*
> *Where spells and charms are real.*
> *By quantum physics or wizard chants,*
> *empower this spell of protection from terrorist.*
> *I call forth energies from above and below,*
> *Protect us from these black hearted terrorist.*
>
> *I call forth the energies of Air,*
> *Carry back these terrorist on Raven's wings.*
> *I call forth the energies of Fire,*
> *Burn deeply these black hearts to depart.*
> *I call forth the energies of Water,*
> *Rage forth and carry them back to their land.*
> *I call forth the energies of Earth,*
> *Remove all resolve by terrorist to stay.*
>
> *Whether you be a child of sun and sand,*
> *If you come to hurt and destroy be gone.*

Return now to the land of sun and sand,
Seek no more to harm and make afraid.
Take thy foulness and depart far away,
Harm none as you depart this land.
Begone black hearts now depart,
Let them experience what they impart.
Leave this place as you found it,
Free of evil and filled with love.

When the emotional peak has been reached, you have the option of sending the spell forth with the following words.

Now I send this spell forth,
Make it so, so mote it be!

Or you can charge a white candle with this highly energized spell so when the candle burns, the energy is released.

I now charged this White candle,
As it burns, empower the spell.

While the White candle has no power to grant as it is only wax. The burning candle reminds us to focus of our objective and to keep it foremost in our minds. We visualize the energy being released which is the important aspect to a burning candle. The importance of the candle color is only in our mind, whatever color we feel good about is the right one for us. One color is not better than another color, unless in our mind we make such a distinction.

SPELL TO ATTRACT MONEY

This spell will attract money to you and is best done when the moon is waxing or on the full moon. Substitute words to better match the method or outcome you desire. The important point is that while you are saying the chant or spell, focus, concentrate and imagine seeing the outcome you are seeking. The better you can visualize the outcome, empowered by your feelings and emotions, the faster the energy peak will be achieved.

> *I enter this magical realm,*
> *Where spells and charms are real.*
> *By quantum physics or wizard chants,*
> *empower this spell I now enchant*
> *I direct this spell for wealth.*
> *Send forth now prosperity and fortune.*
>
> *I call forth the energies of Air,*
> *Give my spell the power of flight.*
> *I call forth the energies of Fire,*
> *Give my spell fiery passion.*
> *I call forth the energies of Water,*
> *Give my spell free flowing.*
> *I call forth the energies of Earth,*
> *Give my spell substance.*

Once the emotional peak is achieved, the power can be released by the following verse.

> *Now I send this spell forth,*
> *Make it so, so mote it be!*

If the spell is created to charge a candle, than the following verses would apply.

> *I now charged this red candle,*
> *As it burns, empower the spell.*

SPELL FOR HEALING DISEASE AND ILLNESS

Spells for the healing of the sick is one of the most sought after remedy by man. In the early days, mountain witches were considered the common folk doctor because they knew so much about herbal remedies and how to treat the ill. Today, we can cast a spell on the waning moon or on the full moon to effect healing. As in all things, the patient should seek the council of competent physicians before they consider turning to magic spells for healing. This is the spell that I have found to be most helpful for us. We are not giving medical advise but we are sharing what has worked for us in our situation. The important point is that while you are saying the chant or spell, focus, concentrate and imagine seeing the outcome you are seeking. The better you can visualize the outcome, empowered by your feelings and emotions, the faster the energy peak will be achieved.

> *I enter this magical realm,*
> *Where spells and charms are real.*
> *By quantum physics or wizard chants,*
> *empower this spell I now enchant*
> *I create this spell for healing.*
> *I call forth energies from above and below*
> *Empower this magic to heal as quick as can be.*
>
> *I call forth the energies of Air,*
> *Carry my spell on wings of doves.*
> *I call forth the energies of Fire,*
> *Give my spell the blazing energy to heal.*
> *I call forth the energies of Water,*
> *Make my spell fast flowing.*
> *I call forth the energies of Earth,*
> *Give my spell strength.*
>
> *I send forth now this spell of healing*
> *to cure _____ of his/her ills.*
> *Rebuild his/her body, mind & spirits,*
> *To restore the health he/she once had,*
> *Now vanquish the illness at once.*
> *All illness turn to ashes,*

All wrongness now is right.
Work thee well now magic spell,
Heal the illness as quick as can be.

Once the emotional peak is achieved, the power can be released by the following verse.

Now I send this spell forth,
Make it so, so mote it be!

If the spell is created to charge a candle, than the following verses would apply.

I now charged this red candle,
As it burns, empower the spell.

SPELL FOR TRAVEL PROTECTION

This travel protection enchantment works best if done when the moon is waxing or on the full moon. The words can be modified to fit your individual situations. The important point is that while you are saying the chant or spell, focus, concentrate and imagine seeing the outcome you are seeking. The better you can visualize the outcome, empowered by your feelings and emotions, the faster the energy peak will be achieved.

I enter this magical realm,
Where spells and charms are real.
By quantum physics or wizard chants,
empower this spell I now enchant
I create this spell for Travel Protection.
I call forth the energies from above and below,
Empower this magic to protect us in our travels.

Protect us in our travel tells,
Guard us against harm and accident.

And the elements of nature,
Or the follies of man, woman or animal.

I call forth protection over our travels,
Let the mechanical parts work well,
avoid the highway dangers as well.

Allow us to arrive safe and sound,
without accident or going aground.
Watch over us day and night,
Work thee well now magic spell,
To protect us in our travel tells.

SPELL FOR PROPHECY

This spell works best when the moon is waxing or on the Full moon. It is a spell to help you become aware of the future. The important point is that while you are saying the chant or spell, focus, concentrate and imagine seeing the outcome you are seeking. The better you can visualize the outcome, empowered by your feelings and emotions, the faster the energy peak will be achieved.

This is a time that is not a time,
In a place that is not a place,
I enter this magical realm,
Where spells and charms are real.
By quantum physics or wizard chants,
empower this spell I now enchant
Now hear me and obey my will.

Help me see what lies ahead,
Fly on wings of an eagle.
Soar high and show me true,
What lies before me

Into the stream of time I cast my thoughts,
To catch a glimpse of what will be.
From stars above to the earth below,
Impart this vision to my mind

SPELL FOR NEW OUTCOME

This spell is for seeking out the best path to travel in our life. It is similar to Prophecy, but this spell is specific for helping delineate your specific pathway in life. This spell works best when the moon is waxing strong or on the Full moon. The important point is that while you are saying the chant or spell, focus, concentrate and imagine seeing the outcome you are seeking. The better you can visualize the outcome, empowered by your feelings and emotions, the faster the energy peak will be achieved.

I enter this magical realm,
Where spells and charms are real.
By quantum physics or wizard chants,
empower this spell I now enchant
I create this spell for seeing the future.
I call forth the energies of the universe,
Empower this magic to show me the future.

In this magick circle well,
Show me the path I must Walk.
Choices many have I,
But choose the one that will benefit me.

A thousand plus paths lies before me,
Outcomes in each are different.
Thy counsel guide me in my quest.
From long ago did you come forth,
Always at my beck and call.

Now show me the path I must follow,
Oh Friend from long ago.

EXAMPLE OF A TYPICAL RITUAL

Be aware of the timing of the lunar cycle for the working of your spells. Waning is good for spells that will decrease and waxing is good for spells for increasing. Waning would be good for spells that are for banishing negative energy or banishing a negative habit or emotion. Waxing would be good for spells for increasing strength, increasing your income or attracting positive energy. Review the section on timing of spells for further information.

Decide if you want to charge a candle so when you burn it, the spell energy is released or if the candle is simply there to help you focus on the task at hand. If you are going to be using a candle, have it in a glass dish or on some kind of fireproof material. Hot wax may run down the candle so take precautions.

Decide if you are going to have some favorite music playing during the ritual. Choose music that bring out the spirituality within you. Hard rock music would not be a good choice for spiritual work. Turn down the music so it provide a soft background sound. Loud enough to hear and sense the spirituality, but low enough to not distract you from your ritual.

We now do the Twenty-to-One approach to lower our brain waves to the alpha level so it will be calm, relaxed and receptive to the programming of the spell. Avoid dwelling on any random thoughts, let them pass though the mind without grabbing onto them. If you lose focus and grab a thought, start over from twenty again. Visualize the descending numbers and nothing else.

We have now entered the alpha state of consciousness and are ready to conduct the purification ceremony. We will recite the Blessing Chant before preceding with the Consecration of the Circle.

Blessing Chant

In this place of power, I open myself,
In this place and in this time I give thanks.
As I seek bounties from thy hand,
I open myself to your divine Essence.
May I see the divine in nature,
nature in the divine and divine within myself and all else.
Oh Great Spirit who guides us all,
I beseech thy bounties both above and below.

Begin by creating a sphere of white light that will protect us from negative energies while the doorway is opened to other realms. The following chant will accomplish that goal. You can change the words around so they better fit your philosophy of life.

While saying these words, imagine with your mind's eye, a blue circle of energy that encompasses yourself and is transformed into a sphere of white light that encloses the circle in a dome shaped energy field. This dome shaped energy field might be considered a force field that prevents negative energy from penetrating.

Consecration Chant

I consecrate this sacred circle of energy,
Open a sphere of white light to protect,
All negative vibrations vanish within.
I invite my spirit guide and power spirits to join,
As I start upon my magic journey.

Recital of the Specific Spell

Perform the spell of choice by reciting it over and over, each time with more emotions and feelings. While you are repeating the spell or chant, envision the outcome you are seeking, feel the energy of having that outcome, taste the favor of your success and hear the outcome with your ears. As you raise in pitch and fever, the words will blend together as one. You will feel the energy peaking and when you do, send it forth or charge the candle. You must focus, concentrate and visualize your desired outcome the entire time you are doing the spell, chant or enchantment.

When you have completed the ritual, you should feel weak as your energy has been spent. This is a natural feeling and it will take some time to recharge yourself. Blow out your candle, unless you have charged the candle, if charged, let the candle burn until it goes out on it own. Depending on what you are seeking to accomplish, if you truly have entered the alpha state, your subconscious mind is acting on the symbols, emotions, feelings, visualizations and imaging.

EXAMPLE OF ROPE MAGIC

In this place of power, I open myself,
In this place and in this time I give thanks.
As I seek bounties from thy hand,
I open myself to your divine Essence.
May I see the divine in nature,
nature in the divine and divinity within myself and all else.
Oh Friend from long ago,
I beseech thy bounties both above and below.

I consecrate this sacred circle of energy,
Open a sphere of white light to protect,
All negative vibrations vanish within.
I invite our friends and spirit guide to join,
As I start my magick journey.
I enter this magical realm,
Where spells and charms are real.
By quantum physics or wizard chants,
Empower this spell I now enchant

I direct this spell to/for _____,
State purpose here.

I call the energies of Air,
Give my spell flight.
I call the energies of Fire,
Give my spell passion.
I call the energies of Water,
Let my spell flow.
I call the energies of Earth,
Give my spell substance.

As you tie your nine knots, begin to say: I can't think your thoughts for you, but you will see mine after each knot. When you have the nine knots, tie the two ends together to make an endless loop.

By the knot of one, the spell is begun. By the knot of two it cometh true. By the knot of three, thus shall it be. By the knot of four, 'tis strengthened more. By the knot of five, so may it thrive. By the knot of six, the spell we fix.
By the knot of seven, the stars of heaven. By the knot of eight, the hand of fate. By the knot of nine, the thing is mine.

Now tie the two ends together to make an endless loop preventing the nine knots from being undone. This is the final nail in the proverbial coffin. Now close by saying:

I tie the final knot that binds all the knots forever, so mote it be.

EXAMPLE OF EMPOWERING A CANDLE

This is an example of a Candle Spell that can be used for removing a person who is causing you problems. The spell will cause no harm to the person, but it will cause them to move from the area and thereby they will stop causing problems for you. We do not want to harm anyone with our spells so we create a spell for relocating the person to another city, far away from you. This satisfies the harm none rule and at the same time provides a workable solution to the problems you are experiencing. We use a white candle, but any color will work as long as you feel good about it.

This same method would be used to charge a crystal instead of a candle. However, with a crystal, it must first be buried in salt for one lunar cycle starting with the full moon to the new moon. This is the waning period when energies are reducing. We want the crystal to be free of prior charges or negativity.

Charging a White Candle

In this place of power, I open myself,
In this place and in this time I give thanks.
As I seek bounties from thy hand,
I open myself to your divine Essence.
May I see the divine in nature,
nature in the divine and divine within myself and all else.
Oh Great Spirit who guides us all,
I beseech thy bounties both above and below.

We consecrate this sacred circle of energy,
Open a sphere of white light to protect,
All negative vibrations vanish within.
I invite our friends and spirit guide to join,
As I start my magic journey.

I enter this magical realm,
Where spells and charms are real.
By quantum physics or wizard chants,
Empower this spell I now enchant
I direct this spell toward _____,
That he or she leave the area completely.

I call the energies of Air,
Give my spell flight.
I call the energies of Fire,
Give my spell passion.
I call the energies of Water,
Let my spell flow.
I call the energies of Earth,
Give my spell substance.

Time now to move on from this area,
Find something else to have happiness.
Move to another city far away,
Packing and leaving right away.
Lose interest in staying in this area,
Abandoned all desires to stay in the area.

We wish him well but far away,
Abandoned this city right away.
Change his heart from being so black,
Let him experience what he imparts.
Begone _____ now depart,
To another city far away.

We now charged this White candle,
As it burns, empower our spell.

As you recite this spell, hold the white candle in your hands, focus your thoughts and visual impressions into the candle. Continue to recite the spell until you feel the intense energy building within yourself. As the energy peaks, focus all of that energy into the candle and pronounce the final two lines of the spell. Whenever you light the candle, the spell will be sent forth to the person it was designated for. When you want to extinguish the candle, pitch it with your fingers for this is the traditional way of putting out the flame.

Parallel Dimensions or Many Worlds Theory

Perhaps the first time you heard about parallel dimension was on a television show, such as Twilight Zone or Outer Limits. Perhaps it was on an old Star Trek show when Captain Kirk was accidentally beamed about another U.S.S. Enterprise in a parallel dimension. Parallel dimensions sound like science fiction to the average person who is not aware of the mathematical equations that support the parallel dimension theory.

How do we know when we have bridged from one dimension into another dimension? Does a bell chime, or does a bright light descend around us? I suspect that we may not realize that we have had a transcendental transition. Nothing goes out of focus and fuzzy and suddenly becomes crystal clear again. We may consider a remarkable healing as a miracle, something the medical profession cannot explain. We may say, "God moves in mysterious ways" but what we are really saying is that we do not understand the physics behind the miracle.

We have yet to realize that this magical transition may be the results of a dimensional shift or in other words, a different outcome is replacing an existing dimension or state of being. This transition may transpire in a slight shift in senses, a minor perception change, because when this time phase shift occurs, we were not fully aware of it happening. We may have missed this transcendental transition completely.

The idea of multiple outcomes at any given moment in time may appear to be far fetched, but quantum mechanics are as accepted as the General Theory of Relativity in the scientific community. New experiments have verified the suggested outcome that Einstein made some eighty years ago regarding quantum mechanics. As scientists seek to tie the general theory and quantum mechanics into one unified theory of physics, we already have laboratory results that have verified that two objects can be in the same place at the same time and can coexist, rather then being annihilated as previously suggested. This simple verification of two objects being able to occupy the same time and space provides the doorway to understanding how two different dimensions could coexist at the same time and in the same space. This remarkable experiment has opened the doors that were previously closed by men of science who was applying outdated and unproven theories.

The more we think we understand about our Universe, the less we really know about it. An atom is composed of electrons revolving around the neutron. We have learned that we really do not know exactly where that pesky little electron is at any given moment, but we approximate the position based on a guess. The huge gape between electrons and between where an electron is supposed to be and is actually at has a lot of empty space in between. We find that there exist a lot of empty space in the atom. This empty space could easily allow the blending in of another atom, especially if the empty space of one atom is filled with the electron from another atom. Thus, our world is filled with a lot of empty space and becomes malleable to subjugation by another dimension that fuses into our own dimension.

Consider the theory of Physicist Fred A. Wolf, Ph.D. in his book, *Parallel Universes* regarding parallel universes and time flow.

> "Gone-by and yet-to-be are simply reference points based on our sense of now. They are simultaneous with us in the parallel worlds view of time. These pasts and futures are…side-by-side parallel universes. The past and future which we remember are just those time wave clashes with greatest strengths and most resonance."

Dr. Fred Wolf visualized the past and future worlds as reflections of our past and future. This concept is like Alice climbing through the looking-glass. If we see subtle differences in the next continuum, it is unlikely we would notice these differences.

The Judeo-Christian tradition presents our reality as a linear continuum, like a flowing river traveling from the distant past to our future. This river flows one way so our past actions are lost and our future actions have not happened yet. Linear time is a product of Western belief, but does not represent the beliefs held by Eastern mystics who consider time a circular function. Some consider this linear continuum as consistent with common sense and experience, but remember that millions once believed that the earth was flat, including the scientist of the day. The history of science is filled with impossibilities. Scientist said Iron ships would not float or the human body could not survive the stress of speeds that exceeded a galloping horse. What they were really saying were that the technical problems had not been resolved. They did not say it was theoretically impossible.

Anyone who states that technology can never get around a perceived impossibility has forgotten the red faces of those who predicted rockets would never work in space because their exhaust gases had nothing to push against. Today we know this was simply a technical problem and not a theoretical impossibility.

The Einstein Special Theory of Relativity suggested mathematically that our past and our future must meet at a single point. We can change our locations in space-time, but our past and future will always move with us as the observer.

Quantum physics has at its heart, the important role played by the action of observation. It seems that whenever an observation of an event occurs, the event will suddenly change, with the results that the event appears to be what we were seeking for and these patterns can act together producing a new physical possibility. This would be like superimposing a number of transparent images in a slide projector can produce an image that is not contained on any of the individual transparencies. Where did this new image come from? In quantum physics, we would say it was superimposed from a parallel dimension. Once the observer takes an action, all possible paths for that action emerge. This is why the Language of Prayer is so effective, once we visualize the outcome we want, all possible paths for that outcome will emerge.

Dr. Fred Wolf suggest that the past and the future must somehow have previously existed as far as our memories are concerned. He reasons that any memory of the past and something we have witnessed in the present is also determined by the future. If the future exist, then where is it? Dr. Wolf suggests it exist in a parallel universe.

Dr. Wolf said, *"Thus it is that the mind of any sentient being that is capable of perceiving a reality is capable of reaching into parallel universes and performing the task of choosing that reality."*

The existence of other dimensions can be experienced in many ways. Consider our own physical evidence. We have what we believe to be documented photographic proof of the existence of parallel dimensions. The dimensional photographs we have posted on our web site cannot be explained away by common camera or photographic flaws simply because they show almost a double image because most were taken with a digital camera which is not capable of double exposing. We believe we have solid photographic evidence gathered from across the nation that clearly show evidence of a duality of dimensions. Beyond our own physical evidence, we have heard from a number of people concerning their own encounters with trans-dimensional shifts.

We have included some examples that we believe suggest a transcendental experience involving a dimensional shift. In some cases, the person viewed into a parallel dimensions and in others, the other dimension replaced their existing dimension. These cases suggest we need to seriously consider the existence of other dimensions beyond our own. *Magic Dimensions* provides the techniques to access these other dimensional realms.

We had corresponded with Laura Olmsted many times by Internet email after writing articles on the *Magic Dimensions* for our Ghostweb Online Newsletter. She gave us permission to use her story about seeking a better outcome for her mother. *My mother spent years sick with a mysterious rash, was on Prednisone and the rash didn't get better, but worse. She was at a point of breaking down early this winter, when I got one of your newsletters and you were discussing finding a place with a better outcome, and so I tried it. I had been exposed to this a little previously, and was certain it could work. It did. I mean, almost literally overnight, Mom went from one huge hive and swollen legs and mental confusion, to a thinner, brighter, happy, alert person with healthy skin, when no doctor had ever figured out what was wrong with her, let alone could find a cure.*

I absolutely believe it had to do with this dimensional reality. I feel that over the past few years I have been drawn into new realizations, and been literally set free from limited beliefs and outcomes. I think that on a daily basis, when a crisis comes up or might, I am able to envision and bring about a different outcome, and I don't understand it, but I feel it and know it works. It worked with my mother, for sure. I believe my relationships, my work performance and own physical health have all been altered by this practice. I know there are other dimensions and we are able to access them, and it's a logical part of living. I think as time goes on people will be even more aware of this and be able to continually enhance our realities by accessing this practice.

◆　　◆　　◆

We met with Linda Pendergrass on a hot afternoon at a local Chattanooga restaurant. While sipping iced tea and enjoying the benefits of air conditioning, she shared her bizarre story of quantum weirdness which seemed to provide the insights into understanding her experience.

In the southern part of Tennessee, where I grew up, there were many caves throughout the area. The closest cave to my house was down the street. It was one of my favorite places. Although I did not go inside the cave, I loved to play around it. I have always been a rock hound and spent many hours there searching for rocks containing crystals and fossils on a hill at the side of the cave. I found so many neat rocks that I brought them home by the bagful! I even found my first arrowhead at this location. My mother was not as thrilled as I was by my good fortune!

One day I had been rock hunting by the cave alone and decided to walk around a while to stretch my legs. I walked to the end of my rocky paradise where there was a small hill, over which led down toward the mouth of the cave through an overgrowth of briars and vines. The spot where I was standing was also at the base of a trail which led over the top of the cave.

As I glanced over the hill, I saw a small freshly dug grave with a wooden cross at its head just a couple of feet from me. The dirt in the small mound was red and beside it lay a shovel. I stood there for quite a while wondering what was buried beneath, a child? Or perhaps someone's pet? As I stood there lost in thought, I suddenly became aware that someone was whistling a tune from the trail which spanned the top of the cave. They were walking toward me because the whistling was getting closer and closer! Instinct told me I might be in danger, so I ran up the street toward my house!

I told my friend, who lived next door, about the grave. She wanted to see it, so I walked back down the street with her later that day. I walked up to the small hill and looked over toward the grave, only it wasn't there! In fact, the area was completely overgrown in vines and briars with no indication that it had been disturbed for a long time. I showed my friend exactly where I had seen the grave, although for some reason it was gone!

I thought it was rather strange that the grave should disappear but, being a child, I soon dismissed it from my mind. However, I did not forget the incident and years later would wonder from time to time about it. Was it a vision from another dimension? I guess I will never know. However, in my mind's eye, I can still see the small grave of red dirt, the wooden cross, and the shovel as it lay there beside the grave after someone's task was finished!

◆   ◆   ◆

Mrs. Shaun-Marie Newcomer relates a tale of a vision of a man who would later become her husband. Was her vision really a glimpse into another future dimension of herself and her future husband? Are there parallel dimensions all around us, and we simply are unable to see them? Mrs. Shaun-Marie Newcomer relates:

I believe that I had a vision of the man who became my husband, about one year before we even started dating. Also, I believe that the power of prayer, coupled with this vision, brought it to pass.

Shortly after taking a teaching job in Savannah, GA I was jogging around Forsythe Park. Ahead of me, but still sort of in my mind (it's very hard to describe), I saw myself in a different jogging outfit and a male co_worker jogging behind me and catching up. As he swatted me gently on my rear then turned and gave me a wide, truly genuine smile. I smiled in return and kept jogging.

The scene faded and I was truly puzzled. Of course I knew this man, he had also just moved to Savannah and we taught at the same school. However, I had just met him and never thought about him in a romantic way. I had no idea if he was even a jogger.

Almost a year after this incident we had become close friends and he expressed an interest in me. I had come to know him as a truly wonderful, honest and spiritual man. We began a relationship and I began to pray to the Lord that if it was His will, we would fall in love and have a long relationship. As I prayed this prayer for the first time, the vision repeated itself in my head and took my breath away. I had forgotten all about it! I took it as a sign that I was "praying" in the right direction.

Even more surprising, was that not only did I find out that he was a jogger, he was a marathon runner. Well into our relationship he suggested that we go jogging together as he was preparing for a local marathon. We went to Forsythe Park (my suggestion, not his) and you guessed it, my vision played itself out in real life! As I was coming around a corner of the park, he came up behind me, swatted me on the rear, and turned to give me the smile I now know so well. I near about fainted and had to stop to collect myself.

This is the first time I've ever told this story. I always thought that folks would find it strange. I never even told my husband (we've been married almost one year) about it. But it proved to me that there were forces at work way beyond this plane of existence.

◆   ◆   ◆

The case involving Anne Marie Jamieson of Glasgow, Scotland is another strange twist involving parallel dimensions. She watched the tragic scene of the assassination of Winnie Mandela on a TV Special News Flash. The assassination take place in an alternate dimension and their TV report of the assassination appeared on the TV in our dimension.

> *When I was about 16 (1986), I was alone in my house studying for my O' grade exams. I was getting bored and switched on television for some background noise. It was about 11AM and the usual morning television shows were on when I heard a mans voice say, "We are interrupting this program for an important news flash!"*
>
> *I looked up from studying my books to watch. The scene on the TV showed a black limousine pulling up in front of a building with a fair sized crowd gathered in front. The sky was dark and the scene switched to the view from the building door. A black chauffeur or usher then stepped forward and opened the left rear door of the car. I then realized that most of the crowd were coloured and it was Winnie Mandela getting out of the car.*
>
> *It was at a time when she was campaigning to get her husband, Nelson Mandela, released from jail. She was wearing a pale two_piece pink suit and possibly a hat to match. The crowd was going daft, waving and cheering, and she started to walk toward the building while waving to both sides of the crowd. Someone then fired a gun three times and Mrs. Mandela fell to the ground, dead!*
>
> *The camera then showed some people running to help her as she fell and some others tackling someone in the crowd (I think it may have been the gun man). It then went back to the TV studio and the newsman who said something like "Shocking scenes" and "The death of a courageous woman, Winnie Mandela, who was campaigning for the release of her husband. "He may also have said where the shooting took place but I can't honestly remember.*
>
> *The TV. then went back to its morning programs as if nothing had happened. This surprised me as it was a live morning TV. show(Rich-*

ard and Judy, I think) and they carried on as if nothing had inter-
rupted their show and not a thing was mentioned.

When my parents came home that evening, I asked them if they had
heard anything about it and they hadn't. I found it strange all day as I
watched all other news broadcasts and this story wasn't mentioned. I
read the papers thoroughly over the next few days and found nothing
mentioned at all, not even an attempted assassination just incase I was
mistaken. It should have made the headlines. I swear I saw her shot
dead on TV. I was even more puzzled when she appeared on TV. a few
weeks later begging someone else for help in her quest. Needless to say
she went to jail some years later (once her husband was released) for
some kind of abuse and as far as I know she is still alive and well. This
whole event has had me puzzled for years but I have an opened mind
and I'm still looking for an answer.

◆   ◆   ◆

At any given time, an infinite number of pathways are available for
us to travel. Imagine walking into a super store and seeing shelves with
thousands and thousands of can goods. All you have to do is pick and
choose the can you want to take with you. The choice is yours.
Another example of this parallel dimensions might be a railroad
switching yard that if filled with tracks coming in from all directions.
All the switchman has to know is which direction you want to go and
he will switch the track for you and your train will change over to new
tracks that will take you to your desired destination. The tracks are
present, all we have to do is throw the switch.

I purchased a British magazine recently because it contained a story
about a man who was involved in an auto accident with his pregnant
wife. Before passing out from the accident, he saw his wife with her
head at an unnatural angle and feared for her life. Upon awakening
from surgery to have bone fragments removed from his brain, he found
his brother was present by the side of the bed. The man asked about his
wife and was told not to worry. Later he was awakened by his daughter

bringing in flowers and a card to him. He asked about his wife and she told him she gave birth just fine. The daughter departed the room and the man stumbles to the doorway and looked out into the hallway, only to discover the hallway was empty. No sign of his daughter.

When the man awakens again, his brother tells him that he is a bachelor and had no wife or children. He called his parents, his neighbors and anyone else who knew him. They all confirmed he did not have a wife or family. The only proof of his not losing his mind is the card signed by his daughter, son and wife.

He somehow was propelled from his dimension where he had a wife and family into a dimension where he was a bachelor. Some may discount this story because of the brain injury, other may suggest that because of the brain injury, he leaped into a new dimension and somehow forces his other self to leap out of that dimension, perhaps into his own. Perhaps they each traded dimensions because of this accident. Interesting food for thought.

I can remember having several dreams in the past of moving through different dimensions and discovering each time that I had a wife and family I did not know. They knew me, but I had never seen them before. I remembered thinking how could I not know my own family, yet these were strangers to me. It is a very odd feeling, to bounce between dimensions, meeting strange women and children who claimed I am their husband and father.

In another dream, I met a son I never knew because in my existing dimension, he was never born. A miscarriage terminated his beginning in this dimension. I had always thought the child would have been a male had he completed the birth process. However, in another dimension he was born with a deformed leg. This "other dimensional son" wanted advice from me on working in the International Scouting Program. I remember thinking that there was no International Scouting Program, but only the Boy Scouts of America. I recommended the Scouting program because I had served as an adult leader for more than twenty years. The interesting aspect is that the son in my dream who came for advice would have been the same age had his birth been allowed by nature in my dimension. When I awakened and told the story to Sharon, she reminded me that I had told her of a son I had lost due to my first wife's miscarriage, years ago. I cannot express the joy I felt at meeting my lost son, even if he lived in an alternate dimension. He was still my son and I was still his father. The interconnectedness of all things, even between alternate dimensions.

What physical evidence exists that suggest this is possible, beyond what our scientist have proven in lab settings? We have several wonderful dimensional photos posted on our web site at Ghostweb.com that I believe suggest this concept of parallel dimensions. In these photos, there are two of the persons in them, not double images, but one person is slightly turned from the other person, one is transparent and the other is solid. It is as if the same person in both dimensions somehow overlaps into one realm at the same time. The bending of the fabric of time and space is not understood by us. Sometimes truth is stranger than fiction. Science fiction of the 1950's has become the technology that we employ today. Science fiction was the bridge to help us realize what may become the reality of tomorrow.

Ghosts, Poltergeist and Apparitions

How do ghosts, poltergeists and apparitions fit into the concept of parallel dimensions? Is there a connection? Our organization, the International Ghost Hunters Society, has been teaching people about the nature of ghosts since 1996. Our teaching goes beyond the rudimentary concepts of things that go bump in the night and embraces the concept that there is life after death. We have taught that ghosts are the evidence of life after death. Our web site, **www.ghostweb.com**, is dedicated to teaching people about life after death or about life in the spirit dimension.

We rejected the concept that ghosts are cursed to roam the earth because they are not in favor with God. We reject the myth that ghosts are demons and therefore evil based on the feeble attempts in religion to have a scapegoat. However, we do accept the concept that if a man was evil in life, he will be evil as a spirit. Evil does not vanish at death, our negative baggage continues with us. It is the evil that men do, not some evil from mythological demons that are fighting a war with God by stealing the souls of men and women on the earth. It is the evil within us and not the evil created by religion. We have to release the negative baggage we each carry, else this baggage becomes an anchor for us and prevents us from evolving to a higher realm. It is the evil that men who embrace religion on a fundamental level like Osama Bin Laden who commit terrorist attacks against humanity, that is evil. Religion justified Bin Ladens' position to destroy the evil of America by sending terrorists to America to blow up the World Trade Center, killing thousands of men and women.

Sharon and I have lived in haunted homes since 1991 so we are no stranger to ghosts and poltergeists and their many antics. We developed an understanding and a love of those who have passed over and were for one reason or another unable to let go of their earthly anchors. The anchors have to be released by them, not by us. Most often spirits have unfinished business or unresolved issues that must be addressed before they are ready to move on from this earthly realm. In such cases, those who claim to be soul rescuers may think their spirits have moved on, but in reality, they must move away from the soul rescuers. They will not leave until they have completion. Those who are simply lost or confused may be helped, but this is not the majority of spirits who remain here. We teach that ghosts are everywhere because they can be found everywhere.

We have helped to establish many ghost clubs and have supported their work by providing a web site that endeavors to contribute knowledge and understanding about the spirits of the dead. While most ghost clubs are simply that, clubs that members join who share an interest in the hobby of ghost hunting, but we have gone farther and deeper into this aspect. We teach that we are a society that helps people to validate the concept of life after death. We teach them how to validate this concept through ghost photography. We teach that new technological tools, such as digital cameras and infrared night vision camcorders, are better then Ouija boards and seances for obtaining valid information.

We teach that the use of scientific standards and protocols are superior to the traditional approach of using self-proclaimed psychics and mediums. We believe that the use of subjective methods, such as psychics, allows for greater misinterpretation of information sensed. We have no way of determining if the psychic is picking up on actual paranormal events or if they are picking up emotional static from their own mind. It has been our experience that most psychics or those who call themselves "psychic" appear to avoid working with investigators who use scientific tools that can validate or deny the psychic information that they claim to obtain.

In our investigations we do not allow psychics to simply paint a wonder picture of who they see, but we demand that physical evidence in the form of electromagnetic field readings, thermal drops or increases, infrared night vision, EVP, digital and film evidence be obtained to validate their findings. Strict Standards and Protocols have been set, to be followed to assure the evidence is credible. We also attempt to discount what we capture or record as a means to eliminate anything that could give us a false readings. We accept nothing at face value, but require that all findings be supported. We have viewed video segments of alleged ghosts filmed in the woods, but no one has gone back to the site and looked for possible sources that might have generated the anomaly. We believe that we must police our own investigations and not allow natural anomalies to be labeled as spirit energies.

For example, the recent destruction at the World Trade Center has produced many still digital photos filled with orbs or tiny spheres. Everyone is jumping to the conclusion that since thousands perished in that terrorist attack that these photos that show hundreds of orbs must be the spirits of the dead. Unfortunately common sense suggests that the amount of suspended dust particles in the air is the source of the multiple orbs being photographed. Just because one does not see the dust particles suspended in the air does not mean they do not exist. This is where the scientific approach provides a better insight than psychics who claim these orbs are all the spirits of those who perished there.

What is the relationship of Ghosts to parallel dimensions? We believe that this question can best be answered by suggesting the following order of events. When we pass beyond the grave, we may leave our physical body in the grave that decays and returns back to the basic elements. That which we call our soul is made up of our essence, who we were in life. The soul retains emotions, intelligence, personality and beliefs. Just as the mind is not the brain, so is the soul not the body.

The soul exists outside the physical realm. The soul is energy that cannot be destroyed at death, but it does transform or evolve at death. The soul, if free of negative anchors will transcend to the closest dimension to us, the Spirit Dimension. The Medium Slyvia Brown has said that this dimension can be as close as three feet from us.

Is this Spirit Dimension "Heaven or Hell"? No, we have found no evidence that this belief survives beyond the grave. The Spirit Dimension or Spirit Realm does not seem to cater to Christianity nor any other man-made religions. This dimension is simply the place that soul transcends into at the time of death where no physical body is required. This Spirit Dimension also appears to be the closest dimension to our own. It is not a parallel dimension, but a separate dimension that is not a mirror image of our own dimension.

In the Spirit Dimension, the denizens are not composed of the lower vibrational matter that we call physical matter, but are composed of spirit matter that vibrates at a higher frequency and is therefore, less dense. This higher vibration is generally not seen in our visual range, but falls within the infrared spectrum and beyond. We have documented that these spirit entities who visit our dimension, can cast shadows when photographed with a flash, yet not be seen by the human eye. Dogs and other animals can see and hear these spirits as can young children. All too often parents suggest invisible companions are only imaginary friends, but perhaps they are the spirits whom the children and see and hear.

Within the Spirit Dimension, the inhabitants may retain their former physical shapes and will create a reality that they are comfortable with, such as houses and buildings that they enjoyed in their earthly life. For example, a man who dies in 1870 may create a reality for himself that is a mirror image of the building and places he knew in 1870. Yet, a man who dies in 2001 may create a reality of the city that he lived within, of buildings or houses that were his in life. His surroundings would reflect a mirror image of his physical life. Is this Heaven? Perhaps to some it might be, but to others, this dimension is a place that dreams come true within. A pious man would create the pious environment that he pictured in his mind. He would be in his Heaven, at least for a time until the reality of his realm is comprehended.

This Spirit Dimension is very close to our dimension, so our electromagnetic and geomagnetic fields would directly attract the Spirit Dimension. During times of peak geomagnetic fields, such as near the full and new moons, the Spirit Dimension will overlap into our dimension causing episodes of poltergeist events to occur as voices and sounds of the Spirit Dimension filters into our dimension. Scenes of apparitions walking about in their time period may be observed, again because of the overlapping of the two dimensions. The apparitions are being observed with in their dimension as it overlaps into our dimension. This cyclic pattern is also influenced by strong solar storms when charged particles bombard the earth. These charged particles are electromagnetic and generate strong fields that can pull the Spirit Dimension into an overlapping state. It indicates the interconnectedness of all things, of which the change in electromagnetic fields can be seen through the use of sensitive equipment.

What happens to the soul that is anchored to this dimension at death because of negative emotional baggage? We can carry with us the emotional baggage that we accumulate throughout our in lives. All of the negative emotional issues that we bury deep within our psyches do not vanish at death, but remain with us as anchors preventing us from transcending into the Spirit Dimension. We must learn to acknowledge and work through those negative emotions that will continue to anchor the soul to this dimension. Once the negative emotions have been released, the soul will vibrate at a higher frequency, thus allowing it to transcend to the Spirit Dimension. The entrance to the Spirit Dimension is not physical, but requires a certain vibrational frequency to enter. Low level spirits anchored to the earth vibrate too slowly to access the higher Spirit Dimension. They are barred from gaining access until they release the burden that is keeping their vibrational level low.

Some souls, once the physical bodies have been shed, elect to remain in this dimension and not transcend to the higher realm. Why? The reasons are as numerous as are the souls who have them. Some souls are content to remain here, they have no desire to depart. Some are anchored here, not due to negative emotions, but due to the love of a place, thing or person. They are not ready to move onto the higher realm, they are happy here and find no reason to depart. They do not exist within the Spirit Dimension, but exist within the same dimension as we do. They may be a little out of phase with us, so we may not always see them, but when geomagnetic fields are peaked, their presence can be heard or felt. Some souls remain near to make certain their loved ones are all right, or they become confused upon sudden death, as in an airline crashing, feeling they are still alive, not dead at all.

Exorcism does not work with the Spirits of the Dead because the icons, rituals or words have no effect on the dead. Exorcism only works with the living who believe and accept the beliefs surrounding the Exorcism. Ghosts do not accept the myth behind the theology, therefore, the exorcism is futile. Another way to view this aspect is that most of the dead were not Christians in life, but were believers of the other world religions which do not accept Christian dogma as being valid.

How do we explain orbs, ectoplasm and vortices that are captured on film and digital formats? We believe that when spirits of the Spirit Dimension visit our dimension they can enter by a doorway or portal opening, such as a wormhole. A dimensional discontinuity that allows spirits to bridge the gap between our dimension and theirs. These spirits are not earth bound, but can enter and leave at will. Their will, not ours. Many times these spirits are deceased family members who return often to check on friends and family members. We teach that many old cemeteries were constructed near these portal sites because of the energies felt by the living at these areas, giving them feelings of being special or sacred.

When a portal opens, intense electromagnetic fields are generated and can be detected with EMF meters. A person standing near by will feel a strong energy engulf them, many report feelings of being sucked into the ground. Others develop migraine headaches, feel light headed and extremely weak. Photographic evidence of these portal openings suggest a circular opening with swirling plasma like energy present. Once the spirits have passed into our dimension, the portal opening closes. We have confirmed this aspect by physically experiencing the portal opening, by photographic evidence and by accounts related by other investigators.

When a spirit enters our dimension, their energy pattern can be captured on film and digital format as a sphere of energy resembling an orb. This orb of spirit energy is generally white, but may be of any color. Our human eyes and mind, at times, will translate this spiritual energy pattern into a human form, but the camera can only record what it detects and according to the physical properties of the film or according to how the CCD array records it in the digital format. The camera does not see what the mind sees, therefore, the mind may see a man standing next to a fence and the camera may record an orb hovering near the fence. Both the film and the mind recordings are accurate, but different according to how the information is interpreted.

An orb can be composed of a single soul or multiple souls traveling as one orb. This arrangement most clearly represents the pattern that might be displayed regarding a collective consciousness. This collective consciousness is a connectedness of all as one. We have a video segment that is posted on our ghostweb.com web site that clearly show an orb is traveling in a horizontal direction and suddenly two additional orbs separates from the first orb and travel a short distance before melting or merging back into the single orb, as it continues in its horizontal direction.

Orbs appear to hover and disassociate their energy, radiating outward as an ectoplasmic vapor or swirl. This appears to take place when the spirit is no longer in motion and is simply hovering or remaining stationary. The collective consciousness concept also applies to ecto-plasmic vapor as multiple orbs appear to be visible at times within this vaporous energy field. The long white streak that is often reported being captured on photographs represents the orb in motion, traveling faster than the shutter speed of the camera, resulting in a contrail pointing in the direction the orb has traveled from. This contrail will appear fainter the further away from the orb itself until the contrail becomes transparent and vanishes from the scene.

Thus orbs are the souls or spirits of those who have lived and died on the earth and who return from time to time to visit loved ones, or those who are anchored to this dimension due to unfinished business, unresolved issues or simply because they elect to remain in this dimension. We have correlated thousands of cases where a loved ones presence is felt, photographs reveals an orb or audio recordings record the voice of the loved one. Why is it so difficult to accept our loved ones once they have passed beyond the veil of this life and return to be near those they love?

How do we know that the Spirits of the Dead do exist in a dimension close to our own dimension. If one were to ask a Christian where Heaven was, could they provide the proper response? Typically Heaven must be in another dimension or in some other place in our Universe. So the question becomes, how do we get there when we die? Some speak of a white light or wormhole that bridges the gap between here and there, but where is there? Based on the numerous sightings of ghosts and our loved ones who visit us, we would have to logically suggest that they are not far. We know that they appear during peak geomagnetic conditions and during times of intense solar storms. Solar storms are due to sunspot activity and sun spot activity is based on the eleven-year cycle. We are back to cyclic influences that trigger what we call paranormal activities, or perhaps a better term might be, Interdimensional activities.

Parapsychologist Jeff Reynolds of North Florida Paranormal Research, Inc., said the following: *The only thing absolute is, that we today are able to get closer than ever, to understanding what makes the spirit world go_round. Clinical study yields little results. Why? Because spirit does not live in a laboratory or test tube. They are among us, the living. Why? Well, here we go again with theories and speculation. Their plane of existence is simply that, a dimension of many levels. For some strange reason, we or they, perhaps both, are able to penetrate the veil separating these two parallel worlds.*

Yes, I said parallel! There are accounts (involved in an investigation now) where people actually hear their doors open and close. Hear, not see! It appears in many instances that the spirit lives in the exact same world we do, only invisible to us. Or is it? Try to explain the movement of objects without using telekinesis. Ghosts put up with our placement of furniture, appliances etc. Why? It's our choice because we have to be here. They don't! Why else would remodeling a home produce poltergeist (noisy spirit) activity when the home had been quiet for many years? They don't accept change any better than we do.

◆   ◆   ◆

Consider the case of Herbert Isaacs who wrote us about his personal experience which we have permission to share. Consider for a moment the question of whether a dream is the subconscious mind pathway into other dimensional realms. For Herbert Isaac, a dream became the vehicle for a transcendental experience that bridged the dimension between his reality and the spirit dimension.

I always wondered if dimensions existed in the afterworld. I know we can get messages many ways from our departed. Dreams and meditation, but really never experienced this myself until three days ago. I have seen my parents in spirit before, but, have never heard in the altered state before. This makes me feel another dimension must exist. I was having trouble getting to sleep, and dozing off here and there. Around four o'clock in the morning, I heard my mothers voice loud and clear. She passed away three years ago after suffering from severe arthritis pain.

She said, "Hi Herb, I hope you can hear me. I'm ok. I am in another dimension. Its just like being alive, but without pain. I am here with your dad, he sends his love, I love you.

◆   ◆   ◆

We have a story told to us by our friend, J. Maciej Trojanowski of Warsaw, Poland. He is a moderator of Paranormal/Unexplained, a serial program on Polish TV Channel TVN. They have been broadcasting since 1997 and have produced over150 episodes. He shared one of their recent on site experience while filming a reported poltergeist activity.

I would like to present to you what sort of work we do for our "Nie Do Wiary" show in Poland. Over last weekend we were filming in Torun, 125 miles North from Warsaw. A beautiful ancient town at Wisla river, birthplace of Copernicus. Further details we promised to keep confidential.

We arrived nine o'clock in the evening on Saturday upon an invitation of viewers of our programme. We were told they hired a house where they have lived for a moth or so. The house was supposed to be an old, 100 years building, what suggested it was mysterious and might have had quite a history. After a week of staying in there, one night our hosts went to bed at 3:00 o'clock. That happens frequently for the women (24) suffers from insomnia. On the back yard of their apartment there is an old children swing made of metal construction. Only a hurricane could move it. Soon after the women heard typical swing creak, that swing creak. She ask her husband if he heard that as well. He confirmed. They thought some stranger entered their backyard. So they looked through the window. They sow nobody, no move of the swing, yet they heard the creak.

Few days later, deep in the night they noticed a shadow moving behind their window. First they thought it was their landlord spying them in the night. Then they noticed that figure, though similar, was sort of transparent. Not in fear yet they looked outside, there was no trace of a human presence.

A number of days passed and one night that happened. They heard a cry of a baby. Just from behind the window of their village house, like if it was coming from the direction of the swing. The cry sound was so clear that the lady could estimate its age as 1,5 to 2 years. They have a daughter that is near three now. When looking trough the window they heard over the swing creak accompanying to the baby cry. As before the swing did not move. It stayed motionless. Near the swing there is a kennel in which a nice, young and friendly small dog spends nights. It is linked by a chain during the night. It started to bark and yap at once. It looked frighten, but soon it turn its behavior. It started to sort of fawn on some invisible creature. There was no wind outdoor. It was quiet warm night. The whole spectacle lasted a minute and stopped, living them in deep confusion. They are believers, though they do not attend church services. The did not watch our programme neither, for they believed they were of rational and lay views on paranormal. First time they become frighten.

The story was completed the day after. Their small daughter, who was just a couple of times taken to church in her live, came to her mother and demanded being taken to church now. It was incomprehensible to them. They decided to leave the place and to move to women's mother place for temporary. The daughter kept asking for going to church for another two days, later she stopped. Each time they visited their apartment they found a window opened though they closed it themselves. After such a visit their daughter for subsequent day or two demands being taken to church. And it has been like that since a month. They went to a priest, who did not ignored their story and gave them exorcize prayers to say. He promised to help, but soon he left for a journey. Eventually they decided to call us and ask us for help.

On Saturday night we were welcome by the husband, who was waiting for us. We drove from Krakow 320 miles to get there. Soon we learnt we were mislead by invitation to come and film, for the landlord gave us no permission to record there. Simply our visit had not been agreed with him. He said he purchased the property on which the house is located some 15 years ago. Indeed there was a 100-year-old house, but in that house lived he himself not his occupiers. The house we came to was stylized for old but in fact it have been only 10 years there. The landlord said there has never been any paranormal manifestation since he owned that property. We were confused. On one hand we had the witnesses and victims, who insisted on their sightings, on the other hand the reluctant landlord, unhappy with our visit for he expected that would bring a bad image to his property.

It had been a long negotiations. We succeeded to get the permission about 12 at midnight. There were three Danish students arrived with us to spent the night in a haunted place. We installed four digital cameras and let them arrange for sleeping. Before we interviewed the hosts who told us their story and showed to us key points on the property.

When my film crew run errands I observed the place and people, fighting with the plaque of mosquitoes. I focused on the small girl, the daughter of our hosts. She was special. She had personality and self_confidence exceeding her age. Specially it was late night and yet she participated in that happening with attention. Like if she new more than she would say. It seemed to me like little Luisa, with her black eyes, dark tan and dirty with earth face, and all controlling view knew very well what was going on there. If anything strange happened there it was always in her presence.

I started to suspect that she was a manifestation of the incarnation of some former entity and she had the ability to trigger apparitions. Unconsciously and unintentionally she terrorized her parents with spirits that she disturbed in peace. I never learnt what was there in that place before, but the new house was elevated on some old foundation. What sort of drama, especially baby drama might had happened there tens of years ago? Aside from the house and the swing there is a little pond deep enough to drawn six foot. men. Who knows what that pond witnessed over the century.

Next morning our Danish friends gave no alerting details. They slept there with no disturbance. Cameras recorded nothing. Was the whole story just an invention? If I was in such a scenario for the first time I certainly would stick to it. With my four years experience I know it was true. To investigate it however more time and endeavors is necessary. The landlord will not allow ghost busting of any sort, so his occupants will leave the house.

◆   ◆   ◆

Imagine hearing the swing creak accompanied by a baby crying, yet the swing was motionless. An explanation might be that the swing was creaking and the baby was crying, not in our dimension, but in a parallel dimension that had overlapped our dimension in which the swing in our dimension was motionless. This strange experience was an example of a poltergeist haunting.

Apparently when the film crew tried to record the poltergeist event, nothing happened. Why? This story presents some typical aspects for the poltergeist noises experienced by this Polish family, but we believe happened when our dimension somehow merged together with a parallel dimension. This blending for a time of two different yet similar dimensions. One dimension where the swing is being used and the other dimension where the swing sits empty.

Consider for a moment the concept of poltergeist. Poltergeist is a German word meaning noisy ghost. Many parapsychologists still believe that poltergeist and in some cases, ghosts, are caused by psychokinesis (PK) discharged by the person experiencing the event. While this may be true for teenagers and for those who have raging hormones and/or elevated emotional levels, for the balance of average people, PK does not offer a viable solution to the paranormal events. Not everyone has the ability to harness that energy to bend spoons with their minds. Instead of blindly labeling all poltergeist events as being caused by PK, perhaps we should open our minds and search for a more scientific and logical solution. A solution that does not rely upon traditional explanations, but a solution based on observable evidence and verifiable results. PK is a catcall, a term that can be used when events are not explainable.

Let suppose that quantum mechanics is veritable as Stephen Hawking has suggested. We have infinite future outcomes existing at any given moment in time. Consider that in one of these other dimensions, a person exists as a spirit. Now lets consider that person creates a mirror image of their earthly home in this Spirit Dimension, complete with bedrooms, living room, kitchen and dinning room. Also imagine that on earth the lunar cycle is near the full moon, which will act as a overlapping trigger.

In the Spirit Dimension, this soul or spirit is moving and stacking boxes in his spare bedroom. In the process of stacking the boxes, one of the boxes crashes to the floor, filling the room with a loud crash. Imagine if you will, that this Spirit Dimension is just a little out of phase with our own dimension. We cannot see the other dimension, but sounds may overlap from the Spirit Dimension to our own. We hear the crashing of a box in the other room. We quickly run to the room, finding nothing out of order.

We credit the noise as coming from a poltergeist, but in reality, the sounds is coming from a dimension that overlapped into our own dimension. No, this dimension is not a place where spirits sit on clouds playing harps and singing eternal praises to their God. This myth dissolves quickly when sufficient evidence indicates that this dimension is typically constructed as the one we live in. When we die, we create the reality we were familiar with while living mortal lives on this physical plane of existence.

What about the apparition of a man who is seen walking through the house, but passes through the wall and vanishes. Perhaps in the Spirit Dimension, he has created his home with the doorway where the wall is in our house. In another dimension, this old house is still standing with the doorway that he is walking through. Sun spot activity triggers an overlapping event and the fabric of time and space overlap as the two dimensions merged as one. Quantum mechanics theory provides an explanation for these kind of haunting experiences being reported on a regular basis. This provides strong evidence to the explanation of why a poltergeist event happens. While the Spirit Dimension is not a parallel dimension, it is still another dimension that exists within the frame work of quantum mechanics.

Understanding quantum mechanics would also explain why the Polish television crew was unable to record paranormal events. The fabric of time and space was not blending or merging between the two dimensions when the television crew filmed the people and the home. The trigger or activation point for the blending of two dimensions may involve the strength of the geomagnetic fields. The geomagnetic fields are strongest at the full or new moons or during the solar storms and flares caused by sun spot activity and from corona mass ejections from the sun that bombard the earth with charged particles.

Western culture believes that when a person dies, they cross beyond the grave and exist in the spiritual realm. We teach in the International Ghost Hunters Society that this realm is a dimension composed of spirits of the dead. These spirits can interface with our dimension when their dimension overlaps into ours, or when they enter our dimensional realm through some kind of wormhole or portal opening that we have proved to exist from our field investigations. These portals are often found near old cemeteries and near other sites, such as Sedona, Arizona and Devils Tower, Wyoming. Both of these sites are held sacred by American Indians who continue to fight legal battles to preserve these sites from encroaching development by builders and by the Government insensitivity to Indian religious sites.

Michio Kaku is a professor of Theoretical Physics at the City College of the City University of New York. He is also author of *Beyond Einstein, Quantum Field Theory: A Modern Introduction* and *Introduction to Superstrings*. Michio Kaku has stated that Scientists have discovered at least ten dimensions beyond our own. It is not science fiction to suggest that the when we die, we pass into the Spirit Realm as Christianity has been teaching it for two thousands years and Mithras cult have been teaching it since BC 600.

We believe that the Spirit Realm, the Spirit Dimension where those who have lived and died on the earth will pass into, is the same dimension that the Christians call Heaven. This Spirit Dimension is the place where the souls who pass beyond the grave emerge within. This dimension must be so close to us that when the physical body is shed, the spirit gains access by some means we are not certain about. This could be a white light, or it could be something as simple as thinking about it and materializing in that realm. The only factors preventing this trans-formation are negative emotional anchors or anchors that require reso-lution before release to the higher spiritual dimension. The important aspect is not how, but that another dimension does exist and can over-lap into our own dimension when stressed by strong geomagnetic fields.

This is the primary reason we discourage individuals from attempt-ing to move spirits along the way by conducting cleansing or other rit-uals to banish the spirits. The spirits have to work out their own issues before they can release those issues and move on. Our intervention does not aid them in this endeavor, but often will hinder that progress. Consider the living, we cannot simply tell someone to stop smoking and expect that person to immediately stop, after years of smoking. We can aid that person only by supporting their decision to stop. They must make that decision and act upon it. Our telling them has no effect and often our comments will prevent them from attempting a change because of human nature. No one likes to be told to do any-thing. Most prefer to have it suggested to them, the decision being their own.

It is a misconception by those in the New Age Movement that cleansing rituals will release the souls. The belief that saying a few words, lighting sage and waving it back and forth will somehow enable spirits to depart this earth plane happy and free. One video segment showed a psychic performing a cleansing ceremony to release the trapped spirits and then a few minutes later she was screaming as she psyched herself into hysteria when the spirits did not vanish at her command. The soul rescuers who boast of releasing thousands of trapped spirits have a really active imagination at best and at worst, they hinder the progress of these spirits.

We have taught since 1996 that spirits are electromagnetic in nature. We were the first to teach that spirits are energy patterns within the electromagnetic spectrum and are influenced by outside EM fields, such as geomagnetic fields or solar storms. Today almost all ghost hunters understand this concept and employ electromagnetic field meters to detect changes in the EMF fields. We also coined the terms, "orb, vortices and ecto-vapor" to describe the ghostly anomalies that appear in our dimension and are known as ghosts. We teach that these orbs of light, vortices and ecto-vapor have intelligence, emotions and personalities. They are not fragmented spirits cursed to roam the earth, but are intelligent entities who have evolved into a higher life form, but still retaining their earthly essence.

About the Author

Dave R. Oester, Ph.D. and Sharon A. Gill, Ph.D. are the cofounders of the International Ghost Hunters Society made up of ghost believers, ghost hunters and ghost researchers. Their popular Ghostweb.Com web site is the largest ghost hunting web site on the Internet. They have been featured on over two dozen television segments, written up in national and international magazines and heard on major radio station across the nation. They have authored two previous books, Trilight Visitors and Haunted Reality. They have authored two home study courses for ghost hunters and paranormal investigators. They are currently busy gathering research for new books.

Bibliography

Barlow, Bernyce 1997
    SACRED SITES OF THE WEST
    St. Paul, Minnesota: Llewellyn Publications

Braden, Gregg 2000
    THE ISAIAH EFFECT: Decoding the Lost Science of Prayer
    and Prophecy
    New York: Three River Press

Brennan, J. H. 1997
    TIME TRAVEL
    St. Paul, Minnesota: Llewellyn Publications

Browne-Miller, Angela. 1996
    EMBRACING DEATH: Riding Life's Transitions Into Power
    and Freedom.
    Santa Fe, New Mexico: Bear & Co., Inc.

Cavendish, Richard, 1967
    THE BLACK ARTS
    New York, New York: The Berkley Publishing Group

Cunningham, Scott 1983
    EARTH POWER
    St. Paul, Minnesota: Llewellyn Publications

Davies, Paul 1995
    ABOUT TIME: Einstein's Unfinished Revolution
    New York: Simon & Schuster

Drew, A.J 2001
    WICCA SPELLCRAFT FOR MEN
    Franklin Lakes, New Jersey: New Page Books

Ellerbe, Helen 1995
    THE DARK SIDE OF CHRISTIAN HISTORY
    Orlando, FL: Morningstar & Lark

Erdoes, Richard & Ortiz, Alfonso 1984
    AMERICAN INDIAN MYTHS AND LEGENDS
    New York, Pantheon Books

Ericsson, Stephanie 1993
    COMPANION THROUGH THE DARKNESS: Inner Dia-
    logues On Grief
    New York: Harper-Collins

Frost, Gavin, Ph.D., D.D. and Frost, Yvonne, D.D. 2000
    THE WITCH'S MAGICAL HANDBOOK
    Paramus, New Jersey: Reward Books

Gill, Sharon A. & Oester, David R 1996
    HAUNTED REALITY
    St. Helens, Oregon: StarWest Press

Gill, Sharon A., Ph.D. & Oester, David R., D.D., Ph.D. 2000
    CERTIFIED PARANORMAL INVESTIGATOR HOME
    STUDY COURSE
    Crooked River Ranch, Oregon: International Ghost Hunters
    Society

Gilmore, Robert 1995
    ALICE IN QUANTUMLAND
    New York: Copernicus Books

Gribbin, John 1998
THE SEARCH FOR SUPERSTRINGS, SYMMETRY, AND
THE THEORY OF EVERYTHING
New York: Back Bay Books

Hawking, Stephen 1998
A BRIEF HISTORY OF TIME
New York: Bantam Books

Hartzell, Harmon, PhD. and Bro, June Avis 1988
GROWING THROUGH PERSONAL CRISIS
San Francisco, California: Harper and Row

Hauser, Nataraj 2001
QUANTUM MAGIC: Mental Meanderings on Quantum Physics and Magic
Circle Magazine, Issue 80, Summer 2001

Jung, C.G. translated by R.F.C.Hull 1974
DREAMS
New York: MJF Books

Kaku, Michio 1994
HYPERSPACE: A Scientific Odyssey Through Parallel Universes, Time Warps, and the Tenth Dimension.
New York: Anchor Books, Doubleday

Knight, Christopher and Lomas, Robert 1996
THE HIRAM KEY: Pharaohs, Freemasons and the Discovery of the Secret Scrolls of Jesus
New York: Barnes & Noble

Knight, Christopher and Lomas, Robert 2001
THE SECOND MESSIAH: Templars, the Turin Shroud and the Great Secret of Freemasonry
Gloucester, Massachusetts: Fair Winds

Kubler-Ross, Elisabeth, M.D. 1997
    LIVING WITH DEATH AND DYING
    New York: Simon and Schuster, Inc.

Kubler-Ross, Elisabeth, M.D. 1991
    ON LIFE AFTER DEATH
    Berkeley, California: Celestial Arts.

LeGrand, Louis E.,PhD. 1998
    AFTER DEATH COMMUNICATIONS: Final Farewells.
    St. Paul, Minnesota: Llewellyn Publications.

Masters, Dr. Paul Leon 1978
    RITES OF THE METAPHYSICAL MINISTRY
    University of Metaphysics

Mathers, S. Liddell MacGregor 2001
    THE KEY OF SOLOMON THE KING (Clavicula Salomonis)
    York Beach, Maine: Samuel Weiser, Inc.

Mathers, S. Liddell MacGregor
    THE BOOK OF THE SACRED MAGIC OF ABRAMELIN
    THE MAGE
    New York: Dover Publications, Inc.

McGaa, Ed 1990
    MOTHER EARTH SPIRITUALITY
    New York: HarpersCollins Publishers

Moody, Harry R and Carroll, David 1998
    THE FIVE STAGES OF THE SOUL
    New York: Anchor Books

Moore, Thomas 1994
    CARE OF THE SOUL.
    New York: Harper Perennial.

Muller, Wayne 1993
LEGACY OF THE HEART: The Spiritual Advantages of a Painful Childhood.
New York: Simon and Schuster, Inc.

Myers, Marvin and Smith, Richard 1994
ANCIENT CHRISTIAN MAGIC: Coptic Texts of Ritual Power
HarperSanFrancisco

Myss, Caroline 1996
ANATOMY OF THE SOUL: The Seven Stages of Power and Healing
New York: Three River Press

Oester, David R., D.D., Ph.D. & Gill, Sharon A., Ph.D. 1998
CERTIFIED GHOST HUNTER HOME STUDY COURSE
Crooked River Ranch, Oregon: International Ghost Hunters Society

Rawlings, Maurice, M.D. 1978
BEYOND DEATHS DOOR
New York: Thomas Nelson, Inc.

Rosen, Eliot Jay 1998
EXPERIENCING THE SOUL: Before Birth, During Life, After Death.
Carlsbad, California: Hay House, Inc.

Sun Bear and Mulligan, Crysalis and Nufer, Peter and Wabun 1989
WALK IN BALANCE
New York: Simon & Schuster

Wilson, Robert Anton 1990
QUANTUM PSYCHOLOGY How Brain Software Program

You and Your World.
Tempe, Arizona: New Falcon Publications

Wolf, Fred Alan 1988
PARALLEL UNIVERSES
New York: Simon & Schuster, Inc.

Index

0-595-22032-0